How to Build a Dune Buggy

By Earl Duty

Copyright 1998 by Amos Press Inc.

Printed and bound in the United States of America

Library of Congress Cataloging-In-Publication Date ISBN 1-880524-26-0

12212460

Published by:

Cars & Parts Magazine, The Voice of the Collector Car Hobby Since 1957

Cars & Parts Magazine is a division of Amos Press Inc., 911 Vandemark Road, Sidney, Ohio 45365

Also publishers of:

Cars & Parts Collector Car Annual

Catalog of American Car ID Numbers 1950-59

Catalog of American Car ID Numbers 1960-69

Catalog of American Car ID Numbers 1970-79

Catalog of Camaro ID Numbers 1967-93

Catalog of Chevy Truck ID Numbers 1946-72

Catalog of Ford Truck ID Numbers 1946-72

Catalog of Chevelle, Malibu & El Camino ID Numbers 1964-87

Catalog of Pontiac GTO ID Numbers 1964-74

Catalog of Corvette ID Numbers 1953-93

Catalog of Mustang ID Numbers 1964½-93

Catalog of Thunderbird ID Numbers 1955-93

Catalog of Firebird ID Numbers 1967-93

Catalog of Oldsmobile 4-4-2, W-Machine & Hurst/Olds ID Numbers 1964-91

Catalog of Chevy Engine V-8 Casting Numbers 1955-93

American Salvage Yard Treasures

Ultimate Collector Car Price Guide

Automobiles of America

A Pictorial History of Chevrolet, 1929-1939

Corvette: American Legend (The Beginning)

Corvette: American Legend (1954-55 Production)

Corvette: American Legend (1956 Racing Success)

Dedication

Over the years a number of people have shared their expertise with me in my endeavors to earn a living as a "mechanic." Among the group is a special friend, Bob "Supie" Supinger, the Volkswagen expert's expert in west-central Ohio. It's doubtful that anyone has repaired more VWs in the past 40 years than Supie. He's a walking encyclopedia with dirt under his fingernails.

Back in the '60s, Supie doctored literally thousands of sick Beetles and vans back to good health in a garage near his home. A dozen or so Bugs and vans scattered around his home awaiting repair served as a landmark and a beacon for those of us who were fresh out of high school and attempting to make a living turning wrenches.

My mentor, Robert "Supie" Supinger, is the man who turned me on to air-cooled Volkswagens from bone stock Karmann-Ghias to super modified dune buggies.

Supie — a dedicated family man, accomplished bowler, and avid mushroom hunter — started working on air-cooled VWs in the early '60s and over the years has taught me practically everything I know about VW air-cooled engines. One of the most important lessons old Supie taught me was that when a particular mechanic's task has become frustrating, just stop and walk away from it before something is broken beyond repair, or before you lose your composure. I can only hope the "old master" is proud of his protege.

Today, we share the same garage space, my shop where I earn a living and where Supie works part-time on his special VW-based projects. Over the years my debt to Supie has multiplied to a sum I'll never be able to repay.

This book is dedicated to the most colorful and likable character I have ever had the pleasure to call "friend" — Robert Supinger.

Thanks, Supie.

Contents

Introduction

Unique People; Unique Buggies

Welcome to the wildly wonderful and zany world of the dune buggy. This all-American invention has provided fun, sport and transport for decades wherever desert, beaches, woods, dirt trails, sand dunes (from which they got their names) and asphalt are found. That's right, the versatile dune buggy can traverse virtually any terrain from city streets to rural woods.

Unlike most vehicles, a dune buggy can be adapted to virtually any kind of operation, from running on the street to mild off-road work to serious mud running to all-out blasts at the local dragstrip. Obviously, building and equipping a dune buggy for these different types of use requires careful planning and budgeting. People in the dune buggy sport are unique, and so are their rides. Their buggies reflect their personalities as well as their intended use.

This book, which has been years in the planning and development, will take the novice through the complete process of specifying components and building his first dune buggy. But it could also prove of interest and use to the experienced builder.

To introduce oneself to the dune buggy hobby, it's advisable that before you buy anything you attend some dune buggy activities, such as

This outstanding dune buggy garnered many admiring looks and for good reason. Both the man hours and expense involved in building this dune buggy had to be staggering. The owner of this pure show machine concentrated the majority of his efforts on the power plant, a highly modified and heavily chromed VW Bug four-cylinder engine.

An excellent piece of engineering work is shown in this impressive buggy concept featuring many design variations utilizing quality components. Even the pro buggy builders were impressed.

Serious off roaders should take a close look at this ride, which has been "built to the hilt" with every off-road option available. Jeff Christensen spared no expense to kick some dirt and bring home the gold.

Fiberglass or metal bodies are both practical and functional, and they look great. The possibilities are endless when you build a dune buggy from scratch. Owner Don Christy, Sheridan, Ind., spent four months building this beauty, which had to be a non-stop labor of love. With adequate skill and perseverance, it shows what can be accomplished in a relatively short time.

runs in the desert, a show, a swap meet, a street rally, etc., and talk to as many buggy owners as possible. This will acquaint you with the various applications available, the different equipment being used in your area, and the types of activities most common in your section of the country. And, in the meantime, visit your local dune buggy shop, or consult various magazines for national vendors specializing in dune buggies and VW parts. Again, shows and swap meets are especially good sources of information as well as parts, etc.

For instance, many of the parts used in our project buggy were supplied by one such national vendor, Larry's Off Road Center, Dayton, Ohio. Proprietor Larry Phillips provided a wealth of technical support and expertise. His brother, Ron Phillips, was also instrumental in providing technical know-how. Located at 4156 Wadsworth Rd., Dayton, Ohio 45414 (phone 937-275-9501; web site www.larrysoffroad.com), the shop offers a full range of dune buggy parts and accessories, machine shop services, and overnight shipping. A catalog lists all the VW and dune buggy parts carried, along with specs and prices. The shop also sponsors several dune buggy and VW activities, among them a major fall event that combines a judged competition for show buggies and a swap meet, and a spring meet that has a show, swap meet and drag racing at a nearby dragstrip.

Again, events of this type are tremendous for beginners and veterans alike. At a recent meet sponsored by Larry's Off Road, numerous examples of finished dune buggies were shown or offered for sale. Present were some excellent examples of a wide variety of buggies ranging from homemade and low-budget rides to high-tech machines with creative engineering and big-buck construction of a professional caliber.

The possibilities are endless when building a dune buggy from scratch. You can select a fiberglass or metal body, both of which are practical and good looking, or you can con-

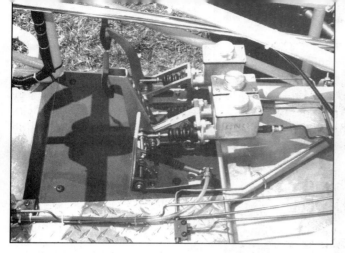

We are considering the use of a stock VW clutch and brake pedal assembly on our project buggy, so we'll scope out this high-tech, state-of-the-art hydraulic system on Jeff Christensen's exceptional buggy, for comparative purposes. This example is excellent in both appearance and function.

For everyday cruising and moderate off road use what more could anyone want than this beautiful buggy. Its owner did an especially good job in selecting body paint and graphics. This buggy is also fitted with a windshield and wiper, and appears to be fully street legal.

struct your own body from a variety of materials, even wood. We see examples of all of these and more at dune buggy meets. The only limitations are one's budget, skills and imagination. You can virtually create anything you want, within reason.

Mechanically, the list of possibilities is endless. Instead of a stock VW clutch and brake pedal assembly of the type we're using on our project buggy, you can go high tech and install a state-of-the-art hydraulic system. You can even mount a power steering system or a tilt wheel, or even four wheel disc brakes.

The possibilities with a dune buggy are unlimited, and a prime example of the upper end is this custom engineered buggy created by Bob Piepmeyer, of Cincinnati, Ohio. He took this buggy beyond the normal limits of design and construction. This buggy has won enough trophies to fill a house, and it's almost done just that; in fact, Bob has reached the point where he has had to throw trophies away. The engine (right) began life as a stock VW Bug four-banger, but Piepmeyer fully customized and hyped the mighty little mill with precision re-engineered pieces, one-of-a-kind parts, and custom fabrication.

Piepmeyer's buggy is unique in that it's equipped with power steering, a stock GM system. And, if that weren't enough, he's also integrated a tilt steering wheel into the setup; talk about pushing the envelope in buggy design! When asked about the time and effort to accomplish all this, Piepmeyer commented, "I've had the buggy approximately 15 years and I find something different to do to it about every year."

While most buggies are powered by a stock or modified VW Bug four-cylinder engine, some more exotic creations sport a small-block Chevy V-8, even a fuel-injected Chevy V-8. Other power options include such candidates as a computer-controlled GM V-6 engine with Tuned Port fuel injection, and even a four-cylinder Ford Pinto engine. In effect, anything that will fit is feasible.

Dune buggies come in all shapes and sizes, and in all color schemes. Again, it's whatever the buggy builder wants.

Some people just love playing in the mud. They'll want a buggy rigged for severe off-road duty, with tires to match. Tires play a big part in the look and function of a dune buggy. Be sure to select the tire that best fits your needs, whether it's drag racing, street use, sand, etc.

When "playing" in the sand, always be sure to have your engine completely sealed against the elements. Just a few grains of sand can

Check out this unconventional buggy featuring wood body panels crafted by John Cole, Vandalia, Ohio. Most bodies are fabricated from metal or fiberglass.

Four wheel disc brakes on a dune buggy? You bet, and they are over-the-counter bolt-on setups. These systems will stop a buggy on a dime and give nine cents change. Hopefully, the guy trailing behind also has four-wheel disc brakes at his disposal.

Being a long time fan of drag racing, I was especially fascinated by this dragster, and quite entertained by its blazing performance. On the 1/8-mile asphalt drag strip, this monster sprinted to an impressive time of 4.87 seconds at 139 mph. Not too shabby for a small air-cooled, four-cylinder VW engine, even if it was modified with such tricks as turbocharging and alcohol injection. Owner Bill Rathbun, Clayton, Mich., takes his fun seriously.

With plenty of power on tap, this pure dragster is ready to blast down the track.

Some people love playing in the mud. When this guy puts the pedal to the metal, you don't want to be anywhere close behind, unless a serious mud bath doesn't bother you.

Different versions of VW-powered earth shakers, such as this asphalt kicker owned and driven by Dave Snyder, New Trenton, Ind., can be found at local dragstrips across the country.

Even stock dune buggies can participate in hot action at the dragstrip, and John Chain, Xenia, Ohio, (foreground) will tell you that it's a real blast.

Even an average guy on a limited budget can build a dune buggy, go to a drag meet or off-road rally, and have a world of fun and excitement. Just ask Ricky Warman, Hillsboro, Ohio.

have disastrous results inside an engine.

A personal favorite of mine among the many and varied dune buggy activities available is drag racing. If you've never been to a drag race, you should experience the sights, sounds and smells of this fantastic sport at least once. Spectators are sometimes permitted to roam the pit area and talk to drivers and mechanics.

VW-powered asphalt kickers can produce some very impressive runs down the strip. At a recent meet, a VW-powered mini dragster covered the 1/8-mile strip of asphalt in a mind-blowing 4.87 seconds with a closing speed of 139 mph. Not bad for a four-cylinder air-cooled VW engine, even if it was an alky-burner with a turbocharger. Even stock dune buggies can join in on the action.

And, of course, there's always the "throttle in a bottle." This is nitrous, and it will provide a rocket-like boost with just about any engine. Just climb in, sit down, buckle up, take off, push the nitrous button, and hold on. It can add from 100 to 150 extra horsepower.

All of this can get quite expensive, of course, but you don't need a fortune or a professionally equipped garage to build a buggy and get into this fascinating hobby. An average

Dune buggies come in all shapes and sizes, as demonstrated in this lineup of magnificent metal.

If this guy's wife ever finds out exactly how much he spent building this beauty, he just might wind up sleeping in it out in the garage.

What a dynamite piece of equipment! No doubt the owner of this rig was an engineer or machinist with access to lathes, mills, etc., and the ability to use them. This dual master cylinder brake setup serves front and rear brakes independently, so if one system malfunctions the other is still operational. The third cylinder (rear) serves the hydraulic clutch.

Bob Piepmeyer, Cincinnati, Ohio, relaxes during a VW and dune buggy show. His super machine is shown in all its glory. It's a guaranteed trophy taker. Note the triple-shock suspension setup, disc brakes, exotic exhaust system and the multitude of chrome-plated engine accessories. When someone builds a buggy like this work of art, he has reached the pinnacle as a master builder.

There are many variations in fuel tanks and mounting locations (right). Some of them are shown here: A fuel cell, the best money can buy, and the type usually found on professional race cars; features an internal bladder that helps prevent the loss of fuel during a mishap, upper left; spun aluminum tank is the most popular type, offered in various sizes and with different locations of the fuel neck to accommodate a wide variety of installations, upper right; another example of the spun aluminum type, showing a different location for the filler neck, lower left; and even an old beer keg can suffice, but installation is a bit more difficult and modifications are required to adapt a fuel line fitting and filler cap, lower right.

Tires play a vital role, both in looks and function. It's important that you choose the tire that best fits your needs, such as: Drag only, available in different sizes and compounds, not legal for street use, (top row, left); Street use, regular passenger car tire with normal highway tread pattern, can be used for light-duty off-roading, such as gravel roads, dirt trails, etc. (top row, right); Mud use, most common variety with deep cleats and heavy duty construction, directional pattern (second row, left); Heavy duty mud use, extra deep cleats, more along the lines of a farm tractor tire, for serious mud use (second row, right); Sand use, front tire, virtually no tread, narrow (third row, left); Sand use, rear tire, paddle type, huge paddle-type cleats for heavy duty sand operation, such as running on loose sand and over sand dunes, also used in sand drag racing (third row, right); Severe off-road use only, deep and thick cleats, extra heavy duty construction (bottom).

guy with limited funds and just normal hand and power tools can do most of what he needs to build a dune buggy, and then take it to the beach, the desert, the woods, or the dragstrip.

Naturally, you won't want to cut any corners when it comes to safety. Be sure to plan on a four-wheel braking system with an emergency brake, a quality fuel storage and delivery system, a strong frame, good tires, quality seat belts, etc. A good quality dune buggy will pass a vehicle safety inspection with no major problems. Most important, it could prevent injury or worse in the event of a mishap.

At a VW swap meet the selection of used parts available to assist you with your buggy project is outstanding. You can pick up anything from a good engine to wheels or anything in between, and usually at very reasonable prices. But, be sure to

If you want to play in the sand dunes, here's a fine example of a well built sand rail. It's owned by David Schuele. CAUTION: When operating in sand and other similar harsh environments, make sure your engine is fully sealed against the elements.

Ever hear of "throttle in a bottle?" Well, this is it! Just push the nitrous oxygen button and pray that you have a long shut down area because you're going to need it with the extra 100 to 150 horsepower provided by NOS.

A vendor at a VW swap meet offers a wide selection of used parts. He's typical of many swap meet vendors, most of whom offer reusable or rebuildable parts at very reasonable prices.

Swap meets offer everything from wheels to complete engines, and everything in between. In this case, a vendor is peddling transmissions, axles, starters, VW fenders, brake drums, electrical parts, steering columns, etc. TIP: Bring lots of cash, as most swap meet vendors are not set up to accept credit cards or checks. Also, if you plan on making your dune buggy street legal, get receipts for any and all parts you purchase.

Found at a swap meet, this VW transmission is a heavy duty bus unit. This unit is scarcer than a regular Bug transmission, but it's much more durable and if one intends to do a lot of serious heavy-duty off-roading, this is the transmission of choice. It does, though, require different axles and a heavier rear suspension.

bring cash, since most swap meet vendors will not accept credit cards or checks. In addition, if you plan on making your dune buggy street legal, get receipts for all parts you purchase. Depending on the state you live in, you may have to prove ownership of key components to get the buggy approved for street use. This is particularly acute with engines and transmissions, which normally have factory ID numbers. If you are raiding a parts car for components, you will want to bring along the title and/or registration of the salvage car when having the buggy inspected. (In Ohio, for instance, one must present all receipts for parts purchased to build the dune buggy being submitted for inspection.)

A whole new world of fun and excitement awaits the new dune buggy enthusiast. And the friendship and camaraderie in this hobby are unequaled in any pastime.

VW people and dune buggy builders are among the nicest individuals I have ever had the distinct pleasure of knowing.

Welcome to our fraternity. ■

Here I'm inspecting a speedometer head that I found buried in a pile of used parts at a VW swap meet. Note the complete VW Bug front end (bottom) which could be used in a dune buggy.

Here, a vendor is offering rear trailing arms (front), internal engine components such as camshafts and valve rockers (right), and used cylinder heads, both single port and dual port (left). Starting at one end of a swap meet, one can virtually buy all the parts he needs to build a complete VW engine by the time he reaches the other end of the meet.

If you don't want to buy your engine a piece at a time, you can buy one complete, such as this single-port engine out of a VW Bug. This is one of the most common dune buggy powerplants, and a good bet for a low-budget buggy project, because it's easy to find, less expensive to rebuild and, like the dual-port engine, relatively easy to work on.

This is a dual-port VW Bug engine, as identified by its twin ports on the intake manifold that mounts to the cylinder head. Otherwise, the engines are quite similar, as seen here.

In checking out used brake drums, watch for cracks, gouges, grooves in the drum surface where the brake shoe contacts the drum, extensive rust damage, etc.

Not recommended: Running without front brakes of any kind. Four-wheel brakes are necessary to provide adequate braking, on and off the road. Use a completely new brake system from front to rear, and always include an emergency brake as a backup.

Larry's Off Road Center, Dayton, Ohio, sponsors an annual dune buggy and VW extravaganza that features a show, swap meet, and drag race. This has matured into one of the finest meets of its type in the country, drawing participants and spectators from several states.

Wheel-standing buggies provide a big thrill for drivers and spectators. This buggy is running a basically stock VW Bug four-cylinder engine with a few aftermarket performance parts and a little creative fine tuning.

"Just point this bad boy to the track for me, Mom," says a potential buggy racer for the next millennium.

A modern mechanical sculptor, Ward Hixon, Columbus, Ohio, poses with two of his special creations. A VW mechanic with 28 years experience, Hixon built his unique works of art from used VW parts.

Hixon's robot and Star Wars pooch are formed primarily from VW engine parts, all of which have been refinished and precision crafted.

The Steps to Building a Dune Buggy

Things to Consider

There are many decisions to make before you purchase anything for a dune buggy project. First, of course, you must determine what type of buggy you want, and to make that decision you must know how you're going to use it. When going through the different decision-making processes, you'll be exposed to a lot of ideas, concepts, different makes of frames, bodies and other parts, various suppliers, etc., so know up front what you want before you start acquiring parts, specifying components, etc.

In the following, we'll explore some of the areas we considered in planning and executing our buggy building project.

Our project dune buggy will use:

- A stock VW Bug ball joint front suspension.
- A stock VW Bug rear torsion and trailing arms.
- A stock VW Bug transmission.
- A rebuilt stock VW Bug 1600 engine.

When purchasing your frame, you will want to consider the type of

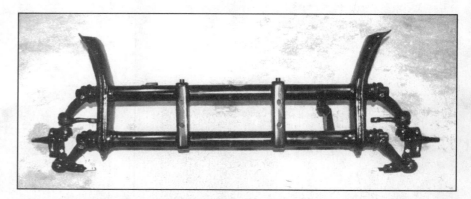

When purchasing your frame, there are many things to consider, such as, do you want a stock VW Bug front suspension, or will you be using a super heavy duty off road type? For street and moderate off-road use, moderate meaning dirt roads, gravel roads or four-wheel-drive trails, etc., a stock VW ball joint setup, as seen here, will suffice.

suspension you want, such as a stock VW Bug front suspension, or a super heavy duty off-road type. For street and moderate off-road use, moderate meaning dirt roads, gravel roads or four-wheel-drive trails, etc., a stock VW ball joint or older king pin front suspension will do the job quite nicely. Remember, though, that the older king pin type suspension is harder to come by in good usable condition. In addition when either of these units is installed on a dune buggy you have very little weight on them to add to the wear factor.

Traditionally, most dune bug-

gies are very light in the front end. On the other hand if severe off road use is your intent, such as jumping logs or rocks or off-road racing with flat out pedal-to-the-metal gusto, then a beefed-up front suspension should definitely be your choice. The reasons are quite obvious, i.e. after sailing through the air you want to avoid coming back to earth with the nose of your buggy digging into terra firma and winding up a mass of twisted metal. This damage happens quite frequently when someone uses a stock unit that was not designed for severe use.

The next decision is whether

Or, an older king pin front suspension will do the job quite nicely. Shown here are a complete used unit (left) and a fully rebuilt system (right). Be aware that the older king pin type suspensions are harder to come by in good usable or rebuildable condition.

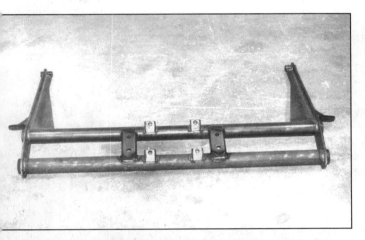

If severe off-road use is your intent, such as jumping logs or rocks, or off-road racing with flat out pedal-to-the-metal gusto, then one of these beefed-up front suspensions should definitely be your choice.

Do you want stock rear torsion or heavy duty off road type? The rear torsion that is most commonly welded into a dune buggy frame looks like this prior to being sandblasted and cleaned. This is a basic VW Bug rear torsion that has been cut out of a salvaged car.

you want stock rear torsion or the racing type.

The rear torsion that is most commonly welded into dune buggy frames is a stock VW Bug rear torsion. The unit is normally welded into place before you buy your frame. If it does not come with your frame, have it installed by a professional welder who has the necessary jigs to properly position the unit in your frame.

Next on the list are the rear torsion arms, and whether you need stock or beefed-up units. Rear torsion arms receive much more abuse than

front suspensions due to the added weight of the engine, so keep this in mind when choosing the rear torsion arms. The stock units work great for street or moderate off-road use, but when really kicking some dirt it is imperative that you use reinforced units. These would have extra steel plates welded on for added strength. There are also units featuring one-piece construction that are used primarily for racing.

NOTE: The super-beefed units install the same way as the stock units without any major modifications to your rear suspension, except

most of the units are manufactured to incorporate the use of at least two, or even three or more shocks. So if you choose these units, make arrangements with the shop where you purchase your frame to have an additional shock plate welded to your rear suspension. Or, if you have welding capabilities you can fabricate your own additional shock plate.

Next, we need to talk about transmissions. VW transmissions come in two basic types, one being the stock VW Bug transmission, or transaxle as it is also called. The other transmission is the VW bus

The unit is normally welded into place prior to when you pick up your frame.

If it does not come with your frame, have the rear torsion installed by a professional welder who has the necessary jigs, to properly position the unit in your frame.

type, which is a larger transmission with beefier gears and internal parts. I opted to use the stock VW transmission. The main reasons for this were:

• Availability - There are many good used units around, and the supply of rebuilt units is quite adequate.

• Price - Good used units can range from $50 on up depending on your source.

• Durability - Since I intended to use my buggy for street and moderate off-road operation, all I needed was a stock unit. And, I have had exceptional luck with stock transmissions. In the six dune buggies I have built, I have not had a single transmission failure, and I have pushed them hard, actually harder than I should have.

If you choose the larger VW bus transmission, here is what you can expect:

• Availability - There were fewer VW buses built than cars, thus there are fewer good used units available.

• Price - When you do locate one, the price is normally higher because fewer units are available and vendors who have good used ones know they are scarce. There are rebuilt units available but with the units being beefier, their internal parts naturally cost more.

A bus transmission from the years 1968 to 1974 is a good heavy duty unit. When checking out good used or rebuilt bus transmissions, look for the three ribs on the top of the transmission. In talking with

local buggy racers this seems to be the transmission of choice, due to such qualities as superior strength and durability. Unless you are a professional buggy racer, going into the many different gear ratios available is not necessary.

A special transmission mount kit will also be necessary to install the bus transmission. The mount kit will install on a stock VW Bug torsion unit. NOTE: Be sure to read the instructions.

Other changes necessary from stock VW bug suspensions are axles and CV joints. The length of a stock VW bug axle is 16-1/4 inches. A stock bus axle is 18-3/4 inches long.

Also, in order to use bus axles, it will be necessary to change rear torsion arms, which are referred to as custom 2x3-inch trailing arms.

If you want to use a bus transmission with stock Bug torsion arms, it will be necessary to use one bus CV joint on the inner or transmission side of the axle, and one VW bug CV joint on the outer or trailing arm end of the axle, plus a torsion axle which is 15-5/8-inches long.

Also when using a bus transmission, it will be necessary to use a shifter adapter because of the added height of the bus transmission. This adapter mounts on the tail stock of the transmission. A good heavy duty clutch set up for a VW Bug engine

Do I want stock rear torsion arms or beefed-up units? Rear torsion arms receive much more abuse than the front suspension due to the added weight of the engine and transmission, so keep this in mind when choosing the rear torsion arms. Pictured here are used stock units, which work great for street or moderate off-road use.

will work well with the bus transmission. Make sure the pressure plate has been matched to the throw out bearing. Your off-road center can assist you with this.

All this might seem to be a lot of work and hassle to use a bus transmission, but if you plan to do some serious off roading it will be money and time well spent.

In respect to another critical component, the floor pan, you can either purchase one or fabricate your own. A dune buggy floor pan warrants proper consideration as it will host a lot of components, including seats, clutch and brake pedals,

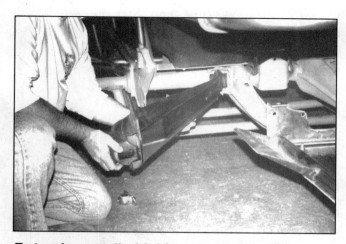

But, when really kicking some dirt, it is imperative that you use these reinforced units.

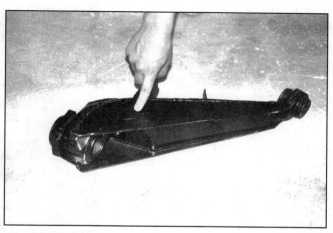

Reinforced units feature additional steel plates welded on for extra strength.

Then there are units with all one-piece construction designed primarily for racing in the dirt or on the strip.

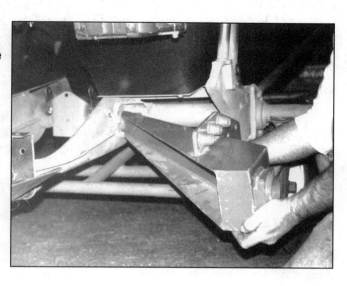

shifter box, brackets, etc. You will need a floor pan that is sturdy in order to meet these needs. On the project dune buggy I used a floor pan that was available from Larry's Off Road Center, and was precut to fit my particular frame. Don't wait until you get your frame home to discover that you should have had additional welding done, such as tabs for mounting the floor pan, additional shock brackets, or light tabs.

If you want to fabricate your own floor pan, you will first need to make a template out of cardboard. Do this by putting the bare buggy frame on its top and laying a large piece of cardboard on the bottom, then tracing along the outside of the

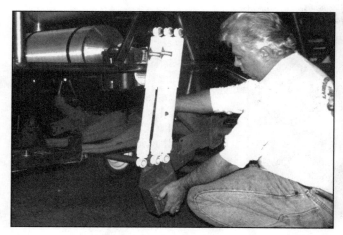

The super-beefed units install the same way as the stock units without any major modifications to the rear suspension, except that most of the units are manufactured to incorporate the use of at least two, or possibly three or more shocks, as shown here by Ron Phillips, of Larry's Off Road Center, Dayton, Ohio.

So, if you elect to add extra shocks, make arrangements with the shop where you purchase your frame to have an additional shock plate welded to your rear suspension. Or, if you have welding capabilities, you can fabricate your own additional shock plate, as depicted here.

frame rails. If your frame has tree bars, do not include them when you trace your floor pan. Make sure that your template is extremely accurate, because the floor pan will be cut to your pattern. If it's not right, you'll end up with a large chunk of scrap metal.

Next, transfer your cardboard template to either a flat piece of steel or aluminum sheet metal and cut accordingly with a saber saw. The thickness of the metal should be at least 1/8-inch thick. If you do not have access to sheet steel or aluminum of this thickness, most metal fabrication shops can supply it. With the proper template, the shop should also have the equipment to cut your floor pan design.

Now that you've selected the floor pan design, you can decide what to do about a body, such as specifying a three-piece fiberglass body, a custom-made metal body, or going naked with no body parts at all.

A number of dune buggy frames have fiberglass body panels commercially available in many different colors. When buying a frame, ask about body panels for your particular plat-

Will you be using a stock VW transmission or a bus-type transmission? VW transmissions come in two basic sizes, one being the stock VW Bug transmission, or transaxle as it is also called.

form. But don't just assume they are available.

A front hood and side body panels do offer very good protection against wind and rocks. The majority of buggies I have seen have not used body panels at all.

But I prefer the protection, comfort and extra security of having a

body around me. However, body panels were not available for my frame at the time I purchased it. But that's not an insurmountable problem either. I simply had a local shop, Waco Enterprises, Sidney, Ohio, fabricate panels out of painted aluminum sheet metal, the same aluminum that is used on oval track race cars.

The next decision "step" in the

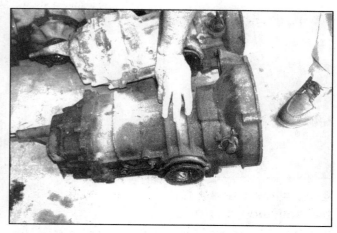

The other transmission is the VW bus-type, which is a larger transmission with beefier gears and internal parts. I opted to use the stock VW transmission for several reasons, including availability, price and durability.

If you choose the larger VW bus transmission, expect to look harder for one and pay more for it when you find it. But you can expect a longer service life from the heavier-duty bus transmission, such as the one shown here. A bus transmission from the years 1968 to 1974 is a good heavy duty unit. When checking out good used or rebuilt bus transmissions, look for the three ribs as indicated in the photo.

dune buggy planning process is another important one, as it concerns the heart of the buggy, the engine. You can either use a stock VW engine or a highly-modified version of the same mill. (Some buggies are even built with non-VW engines, such as air-cooled Corvair powerplants, small-block Chevys, four-cylinder Fords and GM V-6s, but all of these transplants require special adapter plates to accommodate installation with VW transaxles.)

Selecting an engine may be more a matter of finances than anything else. Quite simply, if you are on a limited budget, a good used VW engine may be your only option. Good usable engines can be found at swap meets and in junkyards priced

When using a bus transmission, a special transmission mount kit will be necessary to install the unit.

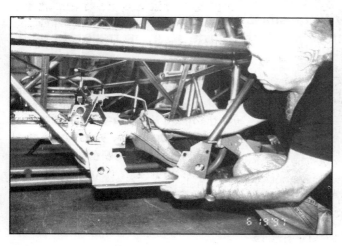

The mount kit will install on a stock VW Bug torsion as shown. Be sure to read the instructions. Other changes necessary from stock VW Bug suspensions include axles, CV joints, and rear torsion arms.

Also, when using a bus transmission it will be necessary to use this shifter adapter because of the added height of the bus transmission.

**Can I purchase a floor pan or will I need to fabricate my own?
A dune buggy floor pan needs serious consideration due to the fact that a lot of components mount to it, such as seats, clutch and brake pedals, shifter box, brackets, etc.**

as low as $150, even less! With just a little clean up and some chrome goodies to dress it up, your used engine can have the appearance of a new one.

If you do buy a used VW engine, by all means put a new crank seal on the fly wheel side of the engine. The procedure for doing this is covered in the engine rebuild section. Also, while the engine is on the work bench give it a good tune-up, such as plugs, plug wires, points, condenser, and fuel filter.

When it comes to modifying a VW engine, the sky is the limit. You can go to extremes, such as having the block bored for bigger pistons and cylinders, or installing high performance cylinder heads, dual carburetors, all out full-race camshafts, high performance ignition systems, lightened flywheels, and the list goes on and on. One of the unique things about air-cooled VW engines is that with very few engine block modifications, such as boring the block and fly cutting the cylinder heads to accept larger cylinders and pis-

**Do you want a three-piece body or no body parts?
A number of dune buggy frames have fiberglass body panels readily available in many different**

colors. But don't just assume they are available, ask your dealer. Body panels were not available for my frame so I had a local shop make some from painted aluminum stock.

Will you be using a stock VW engine or a highly-modified engine? This question might be a matter of finances more than anything else. If you are on a limited budget, a good used VW engine would be the way to go. I have seen good usable engines at swap meets priced at $150 and less. With just a cleaning and some chrome goodies to dress it up, your engine can have the appearance of a new one.

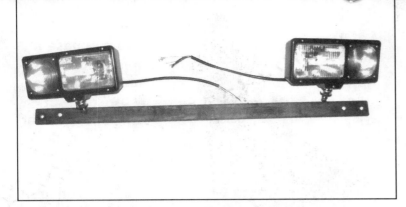

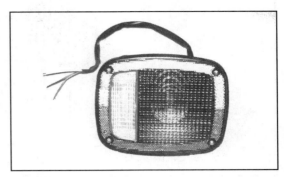

What type of lighting do you want? The lights needed for your dune buggy, such as headlights, rear brake lights, turn signal lights, back-up lights and license plate lights, are easily obtainable at most auto parts stores, discount stores, etc. Always check state and local laws before buying any lighting systems. For my headlight assemblies, I used snowplow lights, which have high and low beams, turn signals and parking lights all built into one compact unit.

The rear brake, parking and turn signal lights are common trailer light units that also fit many truck applications. I turned the units horizontally and used the back-up light bulb included in the unit as a turn signal.

tons, the majority of any other performance modifications are simple bolt-on mods for hiking horsepower.

Also, on the stock 1600 VW engine, you can use a piston and cylinder kit that is 88-mm, which requires no modification to the block or cylinder heads and boosts your engine by 79-cc to 1679-cc.

The next item on the agenda is lighting. The lights needed for your dune buggy, such as headlights, rear brake lights, turn signal lights, back-up lights and license plate light, are easily obtainable at most auto parts stores, discount variety stores or farm implement stores.

The headlight assemblies I used on the project buggy are snowplow lights that have high beam and low beam plus turn signals and parking lights all built into one compact unit. The rear brake, park and turn signal lights are common trailer units that also fit many truck applications. I turned the units horizontally and used the back-up light bulb included in the unit as a turn signal.

Now, how about seats? Dune buggy seats come in many shapes and sizes. The molded fiberglass type is the most common and the most affordable. Molded plastic seats are

also very popular. For all out race seats, you might consider aluminum seats, which are very sturdy and generally priced right. Also available is a super deluxe seat with a tubular frame and lots of thick padding; it's a bit more expensive but the added comfort is well worth the expense.

Also, padded seat covers can be purchased to fit most seats, and at very reasonable prices. Both vinyl and fabric covers are available, but vinyl is generally preferred because it's more water resistant. You can also add extra padding for a more comfortable ride, which is something I highly recommend. I personally wised up to this after some off-road fun left me with a bruised butt.

Moving into the buggy's mechanical workings, there are even options here. For instance, you have a number of options in terms of clutch and brake pedal assemblies. Decent used units are available in salvage yards and at swap meets and usually need just a little cleaning and painted. Salvage or swap meet prices can be as low as $10 for these units, while new stock units available from VW parts suppliers might run as much as $50, and the new breed of high-tech hydraulic units can fetch upwards of $200 to $250.

There are also options in selecting a transmission shifter as there are many types available. Starting with the least expensive are good used units from swap meets or salvage yards. There are also new stock shifters and the premium unit, the chromed high-performance short-throw type with reverse lock-out. Reverse lock-out is very desirable. I have witnessed incidents where improperly adjusted stock units, while being shifted from first to second, would bypass second gear and rake reverse, which can be fatal to a transmission.

There are probably more options with wheels and tires than anything on a dune buggy! Just the selection of wheels to fit a dune buggy using stock VW Bug suspension, whether it uses four- or five-lug wheels, is exceptional. Options range from inexpensive stock rims to several types of exotic aluminum or chrome rims.

After you have chosen your rim type in accordance with your budget, application and personal tastes, matching tires to the rims will be your next step. Here again, the possibilities are nearly endless. For my project buggy, I chose painted spoke wheels all around with truck radial

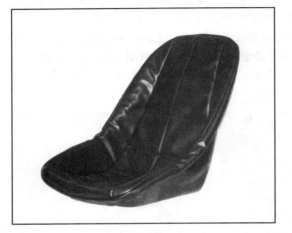

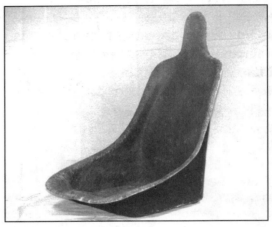

What type of seats do you want? Dune buggy seats come in many shapes and sizes, as reflected in these six photos (at top) of the molded fiberglass type of seat, which is the most common and the most affordable.

Molded plastic seats (as seen in these two photos at right) are also very popular.

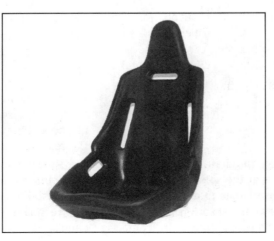

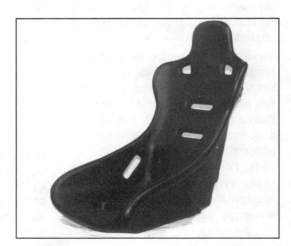

For all-out racing, you might consider these extra sturdy aluminum seats, shown here by Larry Phillips, of Larry's Off Road Center, Dayton, Ohio.

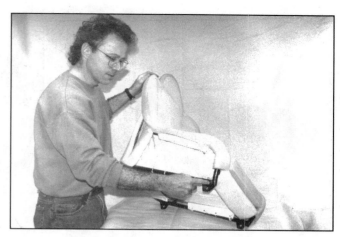

Also available is this super deluxe seat with a tubular frame and lots of thick padding.

Padded seat covers can be purchased to fit most seats, such as the molded plastic example shown here.

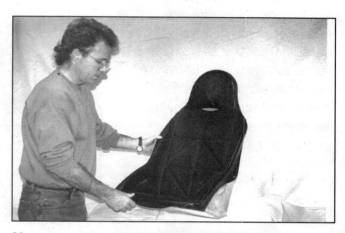

You can even add extra padding to an aluminum racing seat.

tires for the rear wheels and all-season radials for the front. A set of good used tires would work well also. The tire combination I chose is ideal for my application, which, as you'll remember, is street use as well as moderate off-road operation.

If playing in the sand is your thing, then paddle tires will be the hot tip. Without this type of tire, you will just dig yourself a rut in the sand. Paddle tires work great in deep mud also. But for all around off-road use, all-terrain terra tires will get the job done. For a real dirt-digging experience try super swampers, which incorporate extra-deep cleats for maximum traction.

To put some cushion in your sus-pension, you'll need shocks that are up to the task at hand, and that means matching one of the many styles and types available to your specific application. There are inexpensive front shocks available for use with a stock front suspension. A step up from stock shocks would be gas-charged shocks, which can take much more abuse than normal shocks. There are also severe abuse off-road types, such as triple units featuring three shocks in a series on each side.

When purchasing shocks, keep in mind that the sole purpose of any shock absorber is to do just what its name implies, absorb shock when your suspension comes in contact with pot holes, rocks, bumps, etc.

For the project buggy, I opted to use stock VW shocks on the front suspension, since I knew in advance that I would be using my buggy for mostly street running with some light to moderate off-roading. Because the front of the buggy is light, I did not need a stiff shock for my intended use. But for the rear, I chose heavy duty gas-charged shocks, mainly because of the added weight of the engine and transmission on the rear suspension.

However, when doing some off road bumps and jumps, a stiff shock is a must. For such heavy duty operation, a quality system of high-grade shocks is necessary. A set of

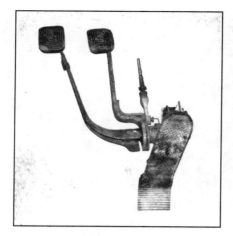

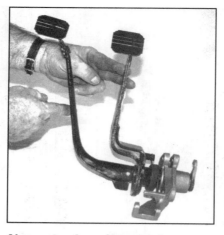

What are your options for clutch and brake pedals? Here you have a number of electives, such as good used units available at salvage yards and swap meets. Usually, all you need to do is clean and paint an undamaged used system and it will work efficiently. Salvage or swap meet prices can be as low as $10 for one of these units in good condition.

New stock units, such as this one, are available from numerous VW parts suppliers.

adjustable coil overs will do an excellent job.

The next decision involves an issue of personal safety, so don't skimp. Seat belts could mean the difference between walking away from a mishap, or being driven away in an ambulance. Safety is always the first consideration and a top priority in selecting any options or gear for your buggy.

Seat belts for dune buggies come in different widths and lengths. Standard sizes are two- and three-inch widths. A variety of colors is also available. You could use a set of belts with adjustable shoulder belts, such as the two-inch-wide type I

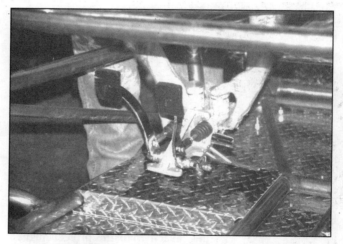

Also available are high-tech hydraulic units, such as the three shown (above, below left and below right).

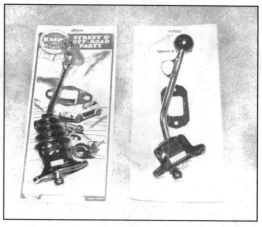

What are your options in transmission shifters? Here again, there are many types of shifters available. Starting with the least expensive, there are good used units obtainable from swap meets and salvage yards.

There are also new shifters available, such as this stock VW Bug unit.

Other kinds of shifters available include the high performance chrome short-throw type with reverse lock-out, such as shown here in two new aftermarket units.

used in the project buggy, or a competition set such as the five-point system so popular with serious off-roaders. Once strapped in with this system, you definitely stay in your seat. If you intend to race your buggy, make sure that any belts you are considering were designed for competition use. There are also shoulder harness pads available for serious off roaders.

Other options available to the buggy builder include:

• Steering wheels come in many sizes and designs. I used a wheel that was not excessively large in diameter to allow easy entry and exit from the buggy.

• Mirrors also come in different shapes and sizes. The type you install on your buggy could range from a small round unit to exotic racing mirrors.

• Steering shafts are available from dune buggy parts suppliers in either chrome or raw steel, which you paint any color you want. It will be necessary to cut the shaft to the desired length and weld one coupler

on the gearbox end. Remember, all welding should be done by an experienced professional.

• Fuel tanks are also an item of personal preference. How you intend to use your buggy will determine the type of tank you want, as well as its fuel capacity. For the project buggy I chose a spun aluminum 11-gallon tank. I considered the fact that my buggy would have a rebuilt stock VW Bug engine good for approximately 22 to 25 miles per gallon, which would afford me a cruising range of 230 to 250 miles on a full tank.

• Choosing an exhaust system is not easy, as the selection of dune buggy systems is mind boggling. Since the rear section of most dune buggies is open with few restrictions, you are wide open in your choice of an exhaust system. I have used both a chrome system and a raw metal exhaust setup that I painted with high-temp exhaust paint. Regardless of which system you use rust will show up somewhere, sometime, but more so on the painted system than the chrome system. This is especially true if you do some off roading or

riding in the rain. If you use the chrome plated exhaust system, there is a special chrome polish and protector carried by most motorcycle shops that helps keep chrome nice in an exhaust application. Some shops with custom exhaust services can build a setup from stainless steel that will never rust, but costs can run quite high, often double a conventional steel system, or more.

• Picking a transaxle strap kit — more commonly called race braces — is relatively easy. For off road race enthusiasts, rear torsion race braces are a must. This support system will keep your transmission secure during those all out race situations where the buggy is being bounced from side to side, and jarred by bumps and hard landings. There are different transmission straps available, such as all steel for the most severe off-road use. This includes an all steel mounting package or the quiet type with rubber covers installed on them. Both of these will also help strengthen the torsion horns. ■

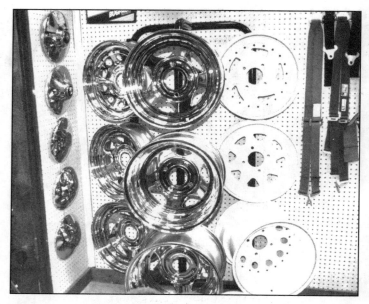

What are your options with wheels and tires? The selection of wheels to fit a dune buggy that uses VW Bug suspension — whether it uses four-lug wheels or five-lug wheels, is exceptional.

You can go from using inexpensive stock rims to many types of exotic aluminum or chrome rims. After you have chosen the type of wheel you want, in accordance with your budget and use requirements, the next step is to match tires to the rims. Here again the possibilities are endless.

For my project buggy I chose painted spoke wheels all around and truck radial tires for the rear, with all-season radial tires for the front. This tire combination works well for street use, as well as moderate off-road use. A set of used tires in very good condition will work just as well.

For general off-road use, these all-terrain terra tires get the job done.

If playing in the sand is your desire, then paddle tires are the hot tip. Without these types of tires, you will just dig yourself a rut in the sand. Paddle tires work great in deep mud also.

For a real dirt-digging experience try these super swampers.

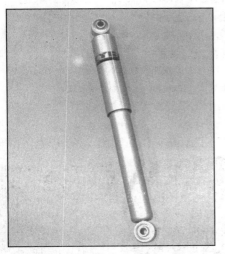

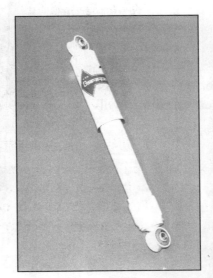

Which shocks should you use? Shocks for dune buggies come in many styles and types. Seen here are five different varieties.

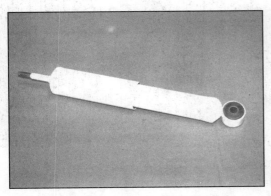

There are inexpensive front shocks available for use with a stock front suspension. For the project buggy, I chose stock VW shocks on the front suspension, knowing beforehand that my buggy would be used for street and moderate off-road use.

A step up from stock shocks would be gas-charged shocks, which can take much more abuse than normal shocks. Considering the fact that the front of the buggy is light, I did not need a stiff shock for my intended use. But for the rear I chose heavy duty gas-charged shocks, mainly because of the added weight of the engine and transmission on the rear suspension.

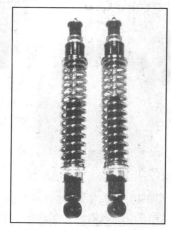

These are severe-abuse off-road shocks, a triple-duty setup using gas-charged shocks. Keep in mind when purchasing shocks that the sole purpose of any shock absorber is to absorb shock when your suspension comes in contact with potholes, rocks, bumps, etc.

When doing some off road bumps and jumps, a stiff shock is a must. A set of adjustable coil-overs, such as the rear shock (left) and twin front units (right) seen here, will do an excellent job.

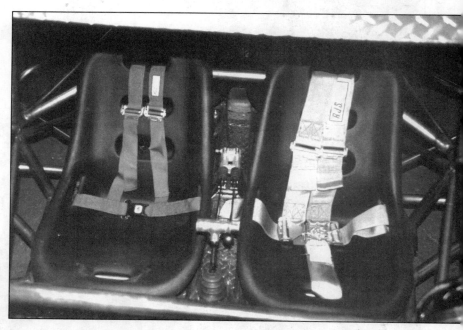

What seat belts should you use? This is one area where safety is a top priority, so don't skimp here when budgeting funds. Seat belts for dune buggies come in different widths and lengths, as seen here; standard sizes being two- and three-inch widths. A variety of colors is also available.

You could use a set of belts with adjustable shoulder belts such as the two-inch-wide type I used in the project buggy (left) or this competition set (right), called a five-point system, which is very popular with serious off roaders.

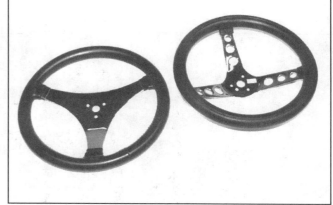

Choosing other miscellaneous parts; what do you want! Steering wheels come in many sizes and designs. I used a wheel that was not excessively large in diameter to allow easy entry and exit from the buggy.

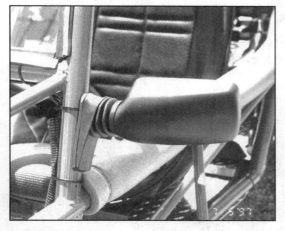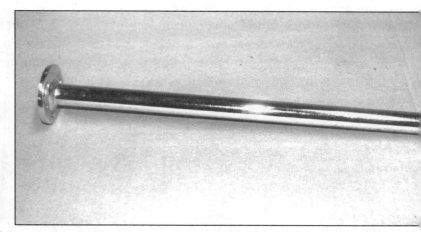

Mirrors also come in different shapes and sizes. The type you install on your buggy could range from a small round type to this exotic racing mirror.

Steering shafts are available from dune buggy parts suppliers in either chrome or raw steel; the latter you paint the color of your choice. It will be necessary to cut the shaft to the desired length and weld one coupler on the gear box end.

Fuel tanks are an item of personal preference. How you intend to use your buggy will determine the type and fuel capacity you will need. A popular style is the spun aluminum tank (left) with center-mounted filler neck. For the buggy project, I selected a spun aluminum 11-gallon tank with left-hand fill (middle). Another possibility is a plain old beer keg (bottom right).

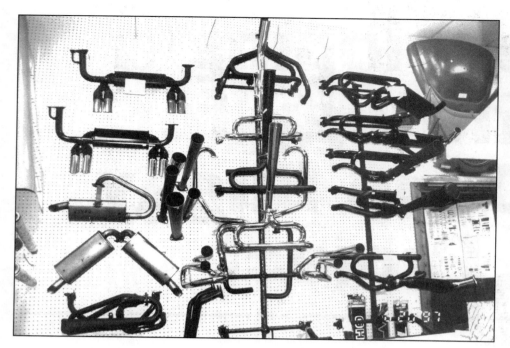

What do you need in an exhaust system? The selection of dune buggy exhaust systems is mind boggling to say the least. Due to the fact that the rear section of most dune buggies is open with few restrictions, you are equally unrestricted in choosing your exhaust system.

How about transaxle strap kits? Also commonly called race braces, transaxle strap kits are a must for serious off-roaders. This support system will keep your transmission secure during those all-out race situations where the buggy is being bounced from side to side while handling bumps and hard landings. There are different transmission straps available, such as the all-steel variety for the most severe off-road use. This includes an all-steel mounting package (above left) or the quiet type with rubber covers installed on them (above right). Both of these also help strengthen the torsion horns.

Developing a Strategy for a Dune Buggy Project

Drafting an Outline

- Locate suppliers for new and used parts

- Choose and purchase a frame - Transport the new frame home

- Build a frame dolly - Sand and paint the frame

- Install the floor pan - Install the horn

- Repair the used front suspension and install it

- Repair the used rear torsion arms and install them

- Install the front and rear shocks

- Install the steering gearbox, tie rods, and steering shaft

- Install the transmission

- Rebuild both rear axles and install them

- Install the brakes, clutch and brake pedals

- Install the clutch and accelerator tubes and cables

- Install the shift box and tube

- Install the front and rear lights, including the light bar and curved rear panels

- Install the storage box

- Install the fuel tank

- Determine seat location and install seats

- Install the starter

- Rebuild the engine and install it

- Install the gauges and switch panel

- Completely wire the dune buggy

- Permanently install seats and seat belts

- With insurance coverage in effect and the dune buggy properly licensed, buggy is driven to alignment shop for front end alignment

- Install body panels, rear side panels, and non-skid tape

Buggy Builder's Tool Chest

The Right Stuff!

The tools necessary to build a dune buggy include basic hand tools and some light equipment that can be found in most home garages, or can be purchased at auto parts stores, hardware stores, and farm supply outlets. Some equipment can even be rented. Here are lists of tools and equipment that will likely be required in building a dune buggy. ■

BASIC HAND TOOLS

- Screwdrivers, both regular and Phillips
- Basic wrenches - Metric 8-mm to 20-mm and SAE from 1/4 to 7/8 inch
- Basic socket sets in both Metric and SAE sizes
- 1/2-drive ratchet and 3/8-drive ratchet
- Side cutters
- Vise Grips - both large and small
- Snap-ring pliers
- Channel lock pliers
- Wire crimpers
- Cordless drill
- Drill bit selection - from 1/8 to 1/2 inch
- Hammers - both small and large, plus a plastic-head type
- Chisels
- Hand-held hacksaw with fine tooth blades
- Brake spring tools
- Allen wrenches
- 12-volt hand-held test light
- Feeler gauge (for valve adjustments) that has a .006" scale
- VW Bug shop manual

SPECIALIZED EQUIPMENT

- Floor jack
- Safety stands
- Bench vise
- Safety glasses
- Safety gloves
- Torque wrench
- Oil seal installers
- Pickle fork
- 36-mm socket
- 1/2-inch-drive impact wrench

SAFETY CHECKLIST: "PERSONAL GEAR"

- Wear work boots; steel-toed are recommended
- Use protective eyewear when grinding, drilling, etc.
- Cover arms and legs when welding, grinding, drilling, etc.
- Don a welder's mask when welding
- Wear gloves wherever possible
- Caps will keep sparks, metal bits, etc., out of your hair
- Masks are required when painting, priming, degreasing, etc.; the respiratory types are recommended
- Don't wear watches, rings, necklaces and other jewelry whenever working on automotive, dune buggy or other shop-type projects

SUPPLIES

- 14-oz. spray cans of paint
- 14-oz. spray cans of metal primer
- Shop towels
- Metal cleaning solvent
- Electrical tape
- Sandpaper
- Scotch Brite pads
- Nylon tie straps
- Wheel bearing grease
- 3 qts. 15w50 engine oil
- 80/90 wt. transmission gear lube
- Assortment of nuts, bolts, flat washers, and lock washers - Metric and SAE
- Brake backing plate lube

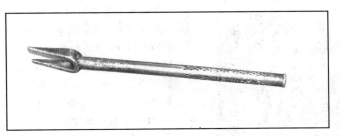

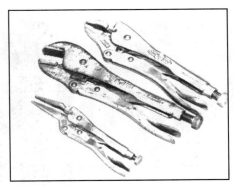

This unique tool is called a pickle fork. The slotted and tapered shank of the fork make this tool an absolute necessity for the removal of upper and lower ball joints on a VW Bug front suspension. The way it's designed to work is, insert the small tapered end of the fork between the ball joint and the spindle, then smack the opposite end with a medium-sized hammer; normally one or two blows are all that's required to separate the tapered ball joint shaft from the spindle.

Vise grips are among the most frequently used tools on any project, especially when building a dune buggy. With their superior locking jaws, these pliers can be used for anything from holding two pieces of metal together, to clamping down on nuts and bolts. Normally, a selection of three different types, as seen here, will cover everything needed on a buggy project.

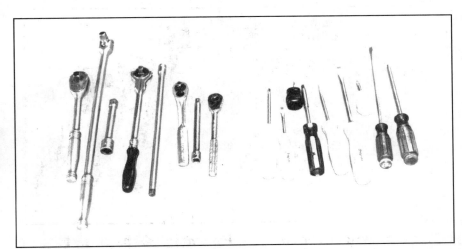

Ratchets and screwdrivers come in many shapes and sizes, and on a dune buggy project we have found that a combination of both 1/2-inch drive and 3/8-inch drive ratchets, plus different lengths of extensions in both sizes, are necessary to complete the job. The 1/2-inch drive ratchet and breaker bar would be used primarily on 1/2-inch bolts and nuts, or any nuts and bolts of larger diameter. The 3/8-inch ratchets are good for practically any other nut and bolt. When the need for a screwdriver came up, we made sure we had an ample supply of both Phillips and the flat-blade type in various lengths and sizes.

A rechargeable or cordless drill with a set of sharp drill bits is a must, (true the drill doesn't have to be cordless, but dragging a cord all over a dune buggy can be a hassle). The drill sizes we used ranged from 1/8-inch to 1/2-inch.

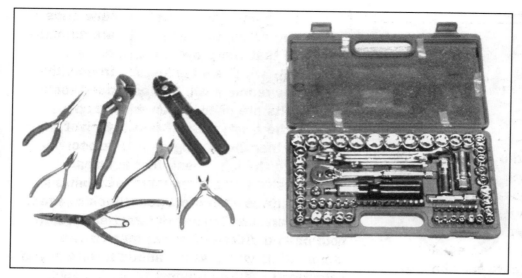

The pliers used on our project buggy consisted of the basic types, such as needle nose, channel lock, and large and small side cutters. For wiring connectors we needed a pair of wire crimpers, and for removing and installing c-clips and snap rings, we needed a set of snap-ring pliers. The different sizes of nuts and bolts one uses will determine the size, type and quantity of sockets needed. The average tool kit that has from 1/8-inch to 7/8-inch SAE deep and shallow sockets, plus 10-mm to 19-mm deep and shallow sockets, should suffice. The options and accessories you choose to install will determine if you need additional sockets.

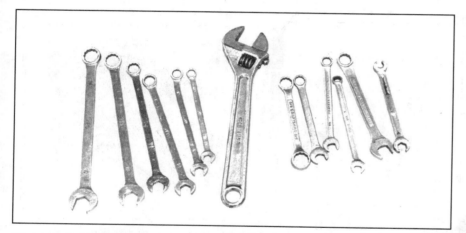

Have a good supply of both SAE and metric hand wrenches at your disposal. Sizes should vary from 1/8-inch to 7/8-inch in the SAE types, also 10-mm to 19-mm in the metric type. A large adjustable wrench will also prove very handy in certain situations.

Hammers will be used to perform such tasks as driving pickle forks to disassemble ball joints, tapping CV joints off axles, knocking old bearing races out of torsion housings, etc. A selection of large, medium, and small hammers will get the job done, and don't forget to include a brass hammer and a plastic-head hammer. Chisels and punches are used for such chores as removing old bearing races or cutting old bolts from used parts.

SAFETY CHECKLIST: "SHOP SUPPLIES"

- First Aid kit
- Fire extinguisher in charged condition
- Phone numbers for poison control, fire department, etc.
- Emergency medical manual

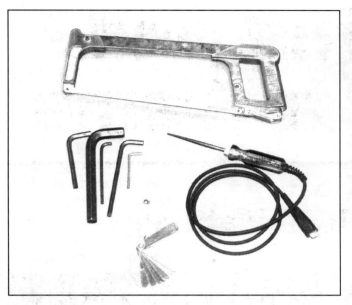

For cutting any type of metal — angle steel, aluminum angle, or round pipe — a hacksaw is a tool that will prove indispensable, especially with new blades. A combination of Allen wrenches will be needed if Allen head bolts are used. When wiring a dune buggy, the trusty 12-volt test light will be your partner for as long as it takes to complete the job. These test lights are inexpensive and can be found at most auto supply stores. One more tool that's needed in your arsenal is a set of feeler gauges; in our case a .006-gauge was all that was required. It was used to adjust the valves on our 1600 VW Bug engine.

SAFETY CHECKLIST: "DO'S AND DON'T'S"

- Never use a tool for a job it wasn't designed to do
- Make sure power tools are properly grounded
- Discard bent, cracked or badly worn hand tools
- Prime and paint only in a well ventilated area
- Dispose of chemicals properly
- Wear chemically resistant gloves when handling chemicals, paints, etc.
- Always wear eye protection
- Watch the sparks when welding
- Keep the eyes shielded from the welder's torch
- Store chemicals in a safe location
- Keep children and pets away from the project
- Don't run the engine in an enclosed structure
- Follow manufacturer recommendations for all chemicals, tool usage, etc.
- Do not store gasoline in an open container
- Do not smoke around a battery or gas tank
- Clean up any oil, gas, or other toxic spills immediately

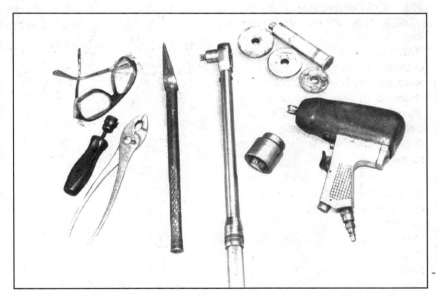

Some additional specialized tools needed on our dune buggy project were a 1/2-inch air-operated impact gun (for those stubborn bolts or nuts); a 36-mm socket to remove and re-install the flywheel gland nut and the rear spindle nuts; a foot/pound torque wrench (for tightening critical nuts and bolts to recommended specifications); a set of bearing, race, and seal installers, (to avoid damage to bearings, races and seals); and brake tools, such as a retainer spring remover and pliers to remove and reinstall hold down clips or springs. And, last but certainly not least, one of the most important tools in any tool box is a pair of quality safety glasses.

Selecting and Painting a Frame

Picking the Right Platform

One of the most important steps in building a dune buggy is selecting the frame and specifying frame options. Critical to this is the selection of a reputable supplier. A good shop with competent personnel experienced in the dune buggy construction can provide the technical guidance necessary to make the right choice for your specific needs.

A good shop will represent several manufacturers and have a wide variety of frames available. For instance, our supplier, Larry's Off Road Center, Dayton, Ohio, had a warehouse full of frames, everything from basic one- and two-seater frames to heavy duty and racing frames. There are even four-seater buggy frames (just in case you want to take the kids along).

When selecting a frame there are a number of things to consider. No matter which frame you choose, an exception being a one-seat-only race frame, you can build it for either street operation, moderate off road running, or off-road racing. If you choose to drive on the street, be sure to build it to meet all vehicle codes, and comply with insurance regulations (check with your insurance agent).

If it is for street use, or for show only, the basic no frills dune buggy frame is a perfect beginning. It is easy to work with and has adequate bracing for strength. When purchasing any frame, don't forget to have

A wide variety of frames is available and the best way to make a selection is to visit a dune buggy/off-road shop. Here, we're visiting the frame warehouse of Larry's Off Road Center, Dayton, Ohio. Not only does this shop stock a wide variety of basic buggy frames, both two-seater and four-seater, but it also has race frames.

Race frames are designed and fabricated for serious off-road use and typically include extra support bars for added strength. Numerous other heavy duty options are also offered with this type of frame (as well as most other types of frames). But since most of this heavy duty gear is factory installed, it must be specified when the frame is ordered.

When selecting a frame, there are a number of things to consider, as this young man discovers while inspecting the finer details of a basic frame. If it is for street use or show only, the basic no frills dune buggy frame is a wise choice.

extra tabs welded on for mounting lights, floor pans, and steering shaft bearings. Don't wait until you get your frame home, get totally involved in the building of your buggy and then realize you forgot to have light tabs welded on. This will be done at the factory, or the shop through which the frame was purchased, if the shop is so equipped.

For street and moderate off road use, the basic dune buggy frame is still adequate. Having extra race braces or added support bars is not an absolute must, but if you think your moderate off roading might get serious, by all means have the extra bracing installed. Racing and serious off-road use puts severe stress on both the buggy and the driver and the extra reinforcement is necessary. Race frames are built for serious off-road use with every option available, including added support bars for extra strength.

Safety is always the top priority in designing and building any buggy frame.

NOTE: It is not uncommon to be racing a dune buggy at a high rate of speed and either be knocked off the track or slide into a corner, lose control and roll or flip the buggy end over end many times. You must have proper protection to walk away uninjured.

For my dune buggy project, I decided on a Pack Rat frame from Bee Line, which Larry's Off Road had in stock. It resembles a mini pickup truck. I chose this frame because it is unique in design and offers the built-in capability of hauling extra gear. On those occasions when you are trail riding for long distances, this extra storage space comes in handy. There are many other frame options available.

On my first dune buggy project I

made the horrible mistake of trying to weld my own frame together. Unless you are a certified welder with proper frame jigs, do yourself a favor and buy the frame completely welded. It will save you a lot of grief and will ensure a strong professional welding job, which is of the utmost importance to the personal safety of you and your passengers.

CAUTION: Never cut corners when safety is at stake. However, should you still insist on doing your own welding, you can purchase your buggy frame in a kit called "tack welded." A tack weld will essentially hold the complete frame together in its partially assembled form. Again, a good professional-quality weld is critical to the safe performance of your buggy.

When you buy a frame completely welded, be sure to specify what type of front suspension you will be using. There are different types, such as king pin, aluminum aftermarket type, or late model VW Bug ball joint type. I will use the latter because of price and availability. I intend to use my dune buggy for moderate off road and street driving so the VW Bug ball joint type will work very well.

After choosing the front suspension to be used on your buggy, the next step is to select the rear torsion suspension system, which also holds the engine and transmission in place. I chose to use the stock VW Bug rear torsion because it is the most common in dune buggy frames, is readily available and has a track record of exceptional performance and durability.

These rear torsion units are normally installed by the frame manufacturer, which has the proper jigs and

When purchasing a frame, it's recommended that you have extra tabs welded on for mounting lights, floor pans, and steering shaft bearings.

This is the Pack Rat frame from Bee Line, the model I chose for my dune buggy project. The frame, which resembles a mini pickup truck, is a versatile design.

Unless you're a certified welder with proper equipment, you should order your frame already welded. If you do elect to do your own welding, you can purchase your buggy frame in a kit called "tack welded." A tack weld will look like this. Essentially it holds the complete frame together in its partially completed form. Don't cut any corners in the welding of the frame; it's just too critical to performance and safety.

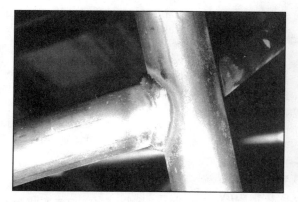

Remember, a good professional-quality weld is of utmost importance to your safety, and your welds should look like these.

After choosing the front suspension, the next step is to specify the rear torsion, which holds the engine and transmission in place. I used a stock VW Bug rear torsion that had been salvaged from a parts car. These rear torsions are normally installed by the frame manufacturer, which has the proper jigs and welding equipment required to make the installation. The torsion assembly is sandblasted and cleaned prior to being welded in place.

The frame I purchased from Larry's Off Road Center had been used for display, so it had been sprayed with a light coat of primer to keep the rust factor to a minimum. Now, how to get it home!

The frame definitely won't fit in the trunk of my car. A full-size pickup works well, or even a mini pickup will work, as these guys proved. However it's hauled, make sure it's fully secured to the haul vehicle. And don't forget to tie a red flag on the end of the frame that sticks out of the truck bed. It would also be advisable to check your local highway codes before hauling your frame anywhere.

When picking up the frame, the first thing I did was to review my checklist and make sure that all of the tabs I had ordered were in place. The frame was exactly as specified.

welding equipment, as well as the experienced personnel, to perform the job efficiently and safely.

Most stock rear torsion systems start out in average used shape covered by years of dirt and road grime. The unit is sandblasted and cleaned prior to welding into place. It will be painted along with the rest of the frame.

When starting from scratch with an unpainted frame or "raw steel" there are a few things that must be done before it can be painted. The reason for this is that steel tubing, such as the type used in the manufacture of dune buggy frames, comes from the steel mills with a coating of oil and grime. All of this must be removed prior to painting or the paint will not adhere to the metal.

Start by thoroughly cleaning the entire frame with a quality metal cleaner, such as a quick dry enamel reducer. Next sand every inch of the frame with a Scotch Brite Pad, making sure to get down into every nook and cranny, especially in the areas of the weld joints. After all the above has been done, go over the frame again with the metal cleaner. If you have access to compressed air, blow the cracks and crevasses free of cleaner and dirt buildup.

For added assurance of a quality paint job use what is called a "tack cloth" to wipe the complete frame down just prior to priming and painting. Tack cloths, metal cleaner and Scotch Brite Pads are readily available at most auto parts stores.

The frame I purchased from Larry's Off Road Center had been used for display, a light coat of primer had been applied to help keep rust at bay. Having made our frame selection, the next task was how to get this chunk of iron home? It definitely won't fit in the trunk of my car.

It's always advisable to check local highway codes before hauling any over-size load. We used a pickup truck with a flatbed trailer to haul the new Pack Rat frame home. But first I checked my list to make sure that all the tabs that I had ordered were in place. Everything was fine. Then the

frame was hoisted onto the trailer and secured to the trailer's tie-down rings with adjustable straps. One final inspection and we were ready to head for home. Once back at the shop, the frame was cleaned and sanded. I started by using a fast dry enamel reducer, but any good metal cleaner will work. The entire frame was cleaned. CAUTION: When using any chemical or cleaning products, make sure you use proper gloves for skin protection, plus an approved face mask to avoid inhaling any toxic fumes.

After a thorough cleaning of the entire frame, I then used a unique metal sanding device called a Scotch

Charles White (left) and Ron Phillips, of Larry's Off Road Center, hoist the frame and carry it onto the open trailer we used to haul the frame home. I then secured the frame down to the trailer with adjustable tie-down straps.

One final inspection and we were ready to roll. It's advisable to cross the straps for extra security; and the use of small axle straps around the frame itself will help prevent scarring of the frame.

Brite Pad. This pad is approximately 4 inches wide x 8 inches long, is very flexible, fits the hand, and fits the contour of any round tube perfectly. These pads can be purchased at most auto parts stores. After the frame had been scuffed completely, making sure that I had not missed any corners or crevices, I then cleaned every inch of the frame again with the quick dry enamel reducer. Next, I touched up the frame with primer where the sanding had worn through the original primer coat. I used a metal primer in a spray can available at any auto parts store or paint store. Then, after it dried, I sanded the frame with the Scotch Brite pad, and cleaned it once

again with enamel reducer. It is highly recommended that a clean, dry cloth, or "tack" cloth, be used to wipe down the frame after it's been primered, sanded and cleaned. This will serve as the final cleaning step prior to painting.

Then we placed a large sheet of plastic measuring about 8 feet by 15 feet on the floor and, placed the frame upside down on the plastic. It's best to paint the bottom of the frame first, in order to preserve the best finish for the top side. Remember, always paint in a well ventilated area and use an approved painting mask or respiratory apparatus. Also, it should be at least 70 degrees in order for the paint to prop-

erly adhere to the metal.

The paint I used came in a spray can and is a common brand name enamel that can be found at most variety stores, farm supply stores, or hardware stores. You can have your frame painted by a professional body shop if you prefer, but I have always had great success using hand-held spray cans. The keys to a good paint job with a spray can are to have the metal clean, dry, properly primered and sanded, and then proceed slowly, applying one coat of paint at a time until the desired finish has been achieved. After painting the bottom, we flipped the frame over and painted the top side.

I had a couple of runs in the paint, so I waited until it had completely dried and then carefully sanded the runs down to the primer coat, using a #400 sandpaper, and resprayed those areas, again one layer of paint at a time.

By taking my time and adding one layer of paint at a time and allowing adequate drying time between applications, I wound up with an excellent paint job. After painting the entire frame, I then sanded, re-primed, cleaned and painted the rear detachable frame bar.

If you're a novice painter like me, you might want to allow at least two days for the complete job, as I did. ∎

Back home, the frame was cleaned and then sanded, as I'm doing here. Only a light sanding was required. I used a Scotch Brite Pad. It was then cleaned again using fast-dry enamel reducer.

Before painting any part of the buggy frame, put a large piece of sheet plastic on the floor. Then place the buggy frame upside down on the plastic, exposing its bottom side.

The finished results, as seen here on the bottom of the frame, were most satisfying. The keys to a good paint job with a spray can are to have the metal clean, dry, properly primered and sanded, and to take your time and slowly apply one coat of paint at a time until the desired finish has been achieved.

There was still a sufficient coat of primer remaining, so the frame was then simply painted. Here I'm painting a piece of the frame. Remember to always start in the corners or crevices of the frame, or frame piece. Also, always wear a mask when painting, and do your painting work in a well ventilated area. A controlled temperature of around 70 degrees is recommended for best results. Apply paint in light coats, allowing adequate drying time in between applications. Spray uniformly to avoid runs. Always follow manufacturer's directions.

After the bottom had completely dried, which required about 24 hours with enamel, we carefully flipped the frame back over so that the top could be finished. By taking my time and adding one layer at a time a few hours apart, I wound up with an excellent paint job.

Building a Frame Dolly

Mobilizing the Project

Once the frame was back in the shop, I decided to build a frame dolly so I could elevate the buggy frame off the floor and have the luxury of being able to maneuver it easily anywhere in the shop.

I started by buying eight 2x4 economy studs and four roller casters from a local lumber yard. I then measured the width and length under the buggy frame and cut the 2x4 studs to fit. The dolly size worked out to be approximately 4x6 feet, leaving me with enough excess wood to extend the height of the upper dolly rail.

With everything laid out on the floor, I proceeded to assemble the frame dolly and install the roller cast-

To construct a frame dolly, you'll need eight 2x4 studs — economy grade is fine — four roller casters, and a box of wood screws. In our project, we elected to use 2 1/2-inch long drywall screws.

We measured the dune buggy frame and then used a power saw to cut the 2x4s into the proper lengths; in our case, that turned out to be 4x6 feet. The leftover wood was used to extend the upper rail. Always be extra careful when using a power saw, or any saw for that matter.

ers, using wood screws installed with a cordless drill. We carefully set the frame on the dolly and prepared to begin our assembly work. ∎

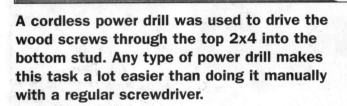

A cordless power drill was used to drive the wood screws through the top 2x4 into the bottom stud. Any type of power drill makes this task a lot easier than doing it manually with a regular screwdriver.

Here I'm finishing the assembly of the basic bottom frame, after which I used the power drill and drove home the screws to mount the roller casters.

The finished dolly ... not necessarily a work of art, but certainly functional, sturdy and a real asset in the project we're undertaking. The use of the frame dolly will make a lot of tasks simpler, easier and safer to perform, as we'll soon see.

Installing the Floorpan

A Visible Means of Support

The floor of your dune buggy is of vital importance, as it supports you, your passenger and your cargo. It is not an area in which one wants to skimp on the quality of the pan or the quality of the installation.

The floor pan for our project buggy came from Larry's Off Road Center, Dayton, Ohio. This is the easiest and quickest way to acquire a quality floor pan, but you can also opt to have a metal fabrication shop cut a floor pan to fit your buggy frame. However, you will have to supply them with a template of your pan made of cardboard.

Making the template is basically quite simple. It requires a large piece of cardboard, or two pieces of cardboard taped together. Then with some assistance, lay the buggy frame either on its top or side. While an assistant holds the cardboard in place, covering the entire bottom of the buggy frame, use a marking pen to trace the outside edge of the frame onto the cardboard. If you had tree bars welded onto your frame, it's optional if you want them included on your floor pan template.

NOTE: If you do include the extra width necessary for tree bars, this will require addi-

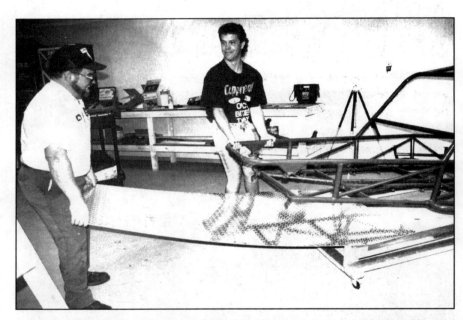

After selecting and acquiring your floor pan and having it painted or treated if desired (diamond-plate floors and aluminum floors are best left unpainted and untreated), you're ready to install the floor pan. Either by using a floor jack or having friends carefully raise the front of the buggy, slide the floor pan in place, being careful not to damage or scratch the paint.

The floor pan I used had been pre-cut to fit the project buggy frame but required a slight trimming of both rear corners, so that the floor pan would fit flush with the rear torsion assembly.

I used a hand-held sabre saw with a fine tooth metal cutting blade to trim the floor pan. Do not drill any holes in the floor pan until the metal has been trimmed to fit the frame.
NOTE: When using any metal cutting tool, be sure to wear safety glasses.

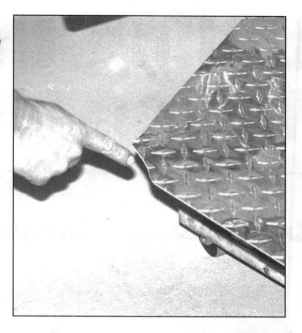

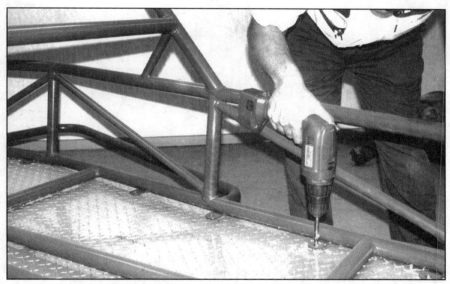

After the floor pan was trimmed to fit the rear torsion system and positioned so that it was evenly spaced on each side of the frame, I then drilled 3/8-inch holes through the floor pan for mounting the floor to the floor tabs. TIP: After drilling one hole on either side of the floor pan, install a bolt with flat washers and a lock washer and tighten securely. This will help hold the floor pan in place while drilling the remaining bolt holes. After all the bolt holes have been drilled, install the remaining bolts, washers and lock nuts and secure everything.

tional material and possibly extra welding by the fabrication shop, which will add to the cost of your floor pan.

After you have traced the outside edge of your frame, remove the cardboard and cut to the outside edge of the trace marks, leaving what should be an exact fit template for your frame. Now reinstall this finished template on the frame and check to make sure it covers the entire floor pan area and that it fits exactly where you want it. When you take your template to the metal fabrication shop, they will cut it to fit that template, and if the finished product doesn't fit your frame, you just paid for a large chunk of scrap metal.

If your frame is painted, and if you have the floor pan painted or are using aluminum or a similar material that does not require painting, you are ready to install the floor pan. Either by using a floor jack or having your assistants raise the front of the buggy, slide the floor pan in place being careful not to damage or scratch the paint. The floor pan I purchased required a slight trimming of both rear corners to be able to slide the floor pan all the way flush with the rear torsion system. I used a hand held sabre saw with a fine tooth metal cutting blade to trim the floor pan.

NOTE: Do not drill any holes in the floor pan until the metal has been trimmed to fit the frame. And, when using any metal cutting tool be sure to wear safety glasses.

After the floor pan was trimmed to fit the rear torsion system and positioned correctly so that it was evenly spaced on each side of the frame, I drilled 3/8-inch holes through the floor pan for mounting to the floor tabs. After drilling one hole on either side of the floor pan, install a bolt with flat washers and a lock washer and tighten securely. This will help hold the floor pan in place while drilling the remaining bolt holes. After all the bolt holes have been drilled, install the remaining bolts, washers and lock nuts and secure the pan to the frame. ■

Repairing and Installing the Rear Torsion Arms

Smoothing Out the Road and Trail

Rear torsion arms are critically important components of any dune buggy, as they are vital to vehicle control, stability and operation, especially on uneven surfaces and rough terrain. They are also critical to rear-wheel alignment. In fact, if they're dented or warped, it is impossible to accurately align the rear wheels.

Consequently, it's extremely important to have them in very good working order. Our dune buggy was intended and designed for street and moderate off-road use, so stock VW Bug torsion arms were ideal for our project. The used torsion arms that we rebuilt were from a 1973 VW Bug. Good used units are readily available at VW swap meets.

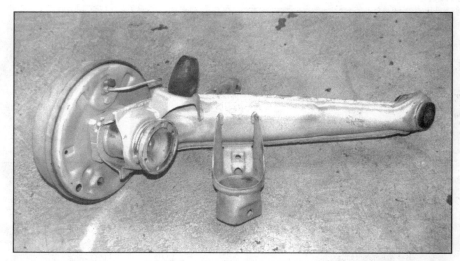

In rebuilding used torsion arms (in our case, ones from a '73 VW Bug), a good beginning for reworking either right or left rear torsion arm assemblies is to leave the brake drums and stub axles on the torsion arms, and send them out for sandblasting. It takes longer and more physical effort, but wire brushes and persistence can also get the job done.

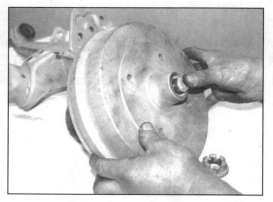

When they came back from being sandblasted, they were ready for disassembly, inspection and repair. Roy Owens started the disassembly by removing the spindle nut (left) and then the brake drum (right).

Next he removed the backing plate retainer bolts (right), and then the retaining cover (below, left), along with the backing plate (below, right).

After removal, our units were carefully inspected for any serious rust or physical damage, such as warping or dents. NOTE: Surface rust on used units is quite normal and not a serious problem. If your budget permits, rebuilt units, both stock and heavy duty, are also available off the shelf. New units can be purchased with or without bearings, seals and stub axles.

The installation process is basically the same for both sides. The accompanying photos illustrate the rebuilding and installation procedures. ■

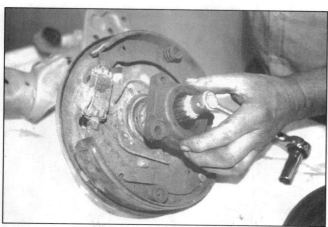

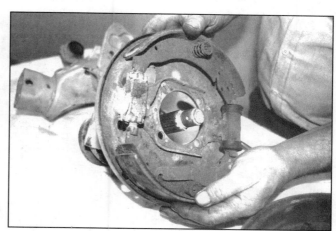

He then used a brass hammer and tapped on the threaded end of the stub axle to remove it from the torsion arm (left). He then pulled it free (right). NOTE: To avoid damage to the threaded end of the stub axle, use only a brass hammer or a block of hardwood placed on the threaded end to tap the stub axle out.

After the stub axle was out, he removed the outer bearing and race, plus the inner spacer.

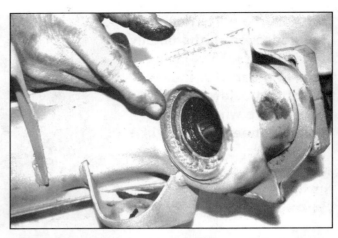

With the stub axle out, the inner bearing seal is now visible.

Roy Owens then removed the inner seal, exposing the bearing and snap ring.

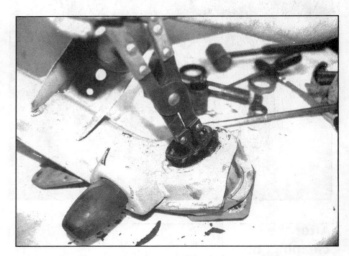

This retaining ring requires the use of heavy duty snap-ring pliers for removal. Here, Roy inserts the pliers into the snap ring and fully compresses the ring.

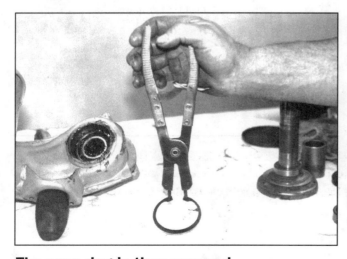

The snap ring is then removed.

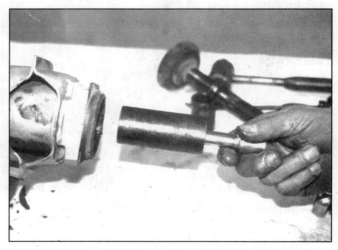

A large deep-well socket with an extension is used to drive the old bearing out of the torsion housing.

With all the parts removed he proceeded to thoroughly clean them with cleaning fluid in a parts washer (right and below left), and with a wire wheel on a bench grinder (lower right).

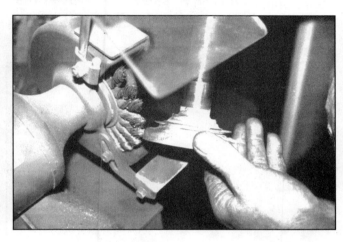

After the cleaning, he carefully inspected both bearings and races for signs of pitting or abnormal wear.

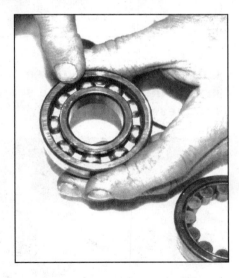

There were obvious signs of bearing wear on this bearing roller.

Note the excessive wear on this bearing race.

We opted to use new bearings in the reassembly of the stub axle. With everything cleaned and ready, Roy repacked both bearings with a quality wheel bearing grease (right; below left; and below right). We chose to use a wheel bearing grease designed for use in boat trailers because of its excellent lubricating abilities.

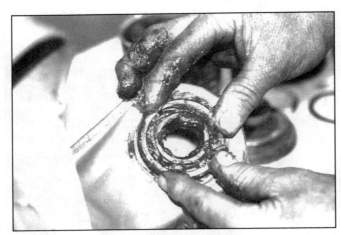

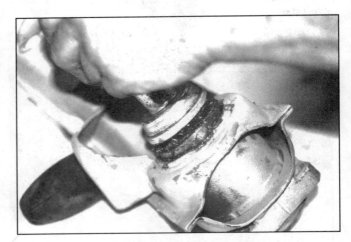

Roy then inserted the inner bearing into the housing.

He used a bearing installation tool to properly seat it.

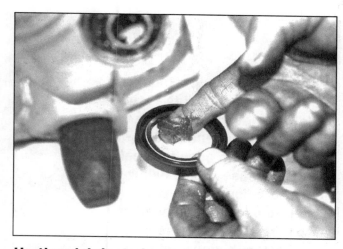

Next came the installation of the retaining ring, again using the snap-ring pliers.

He then lubricated a new grease seal.

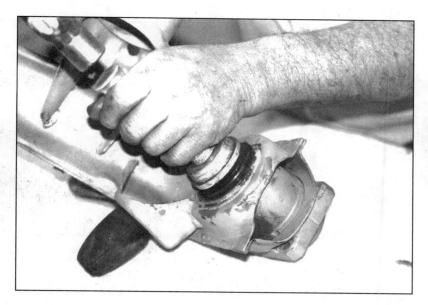

He proceeded to set it in place, and gently tapped it in with the bearing installation tool and a small hammer.

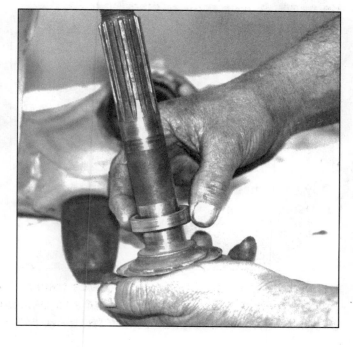

Next, he installed the inner seal race on the axle shaft with the chamfered side (above) pointing toward the large round end of the axle shaft (right).

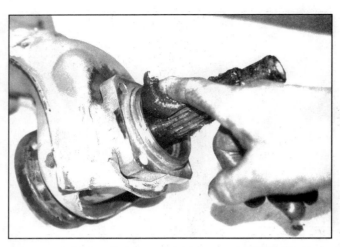

He then applied a small amount of lubrication to the seal race before inserting the axle and race through the center of the inner bearing. Then he used a block of wood (to avoid damage to the axle) to tap the axle in place.

Roy then puts extra bearing grease into the torsion housing and around the axle shaft.

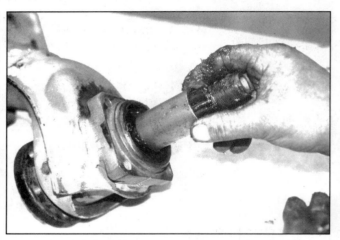

He carefully inserted the long inner bearing spacer.

He followed by installing the outer bearing.

He then tapped the bearing into place (above left), and then installed the outer bearing race (above right). (The outer cover, seal and seal race will be installed later on in the brake chapter in the section pertaining to the rear brakes.)

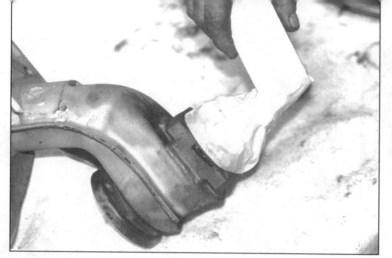

The rear torsion arm is now ready to be wiped clean of excess grease and oil prior to painting, but first Roy tapes the axle shaft and bearings to avoid getting solvent on them prior to cleaning and painting.

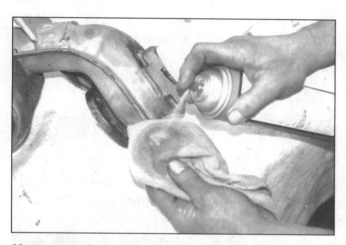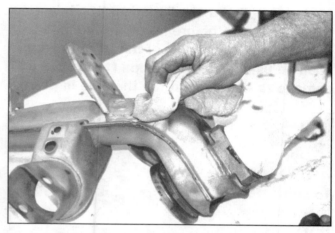

He sprayed cleaning solvent on a shop rag (left) and cleaned the entire surface (right).

When the torsion arm was dry, Roy Owens gave the entire arm four to five coats of semi-gloss black paint. Remember, always wear a mask when painting. The better the mask, the better the protection.

With our torsion arm looking like a new one, it was time to install it into the torsion housing.

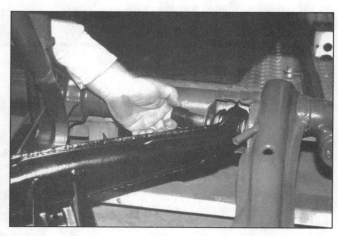

To install the torsion arm, we inserted the small end of the arm, with the rubber bushing, into the rear torsion housing (above left). Then we inserted the retaining bolt (above right). **NOTE: There is a flat washer that goes on each side of the rubber bushing before installing the torsion bolt.**

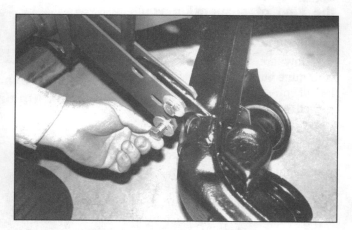

The torsion bolt requires a 17-mm Allen wrench to secure it, although we used an Allen socket.

After our torsion arm was in place and secured by the torsion bolt, we proceeded to install the outer torsion bolts through the torsion arm and the torsion plate. NOTE: Use industrial strength bolts in this area. Now that we had completed one side of the rear torsion arm assembly, we moved on to the other used torsion arm and performed the same procedure.

Selecting and Installing the Front Suspension

Keeping the Bounce Out of your Buggy

Now it's time to select a front suspension for your buggy. This is not as simple as going to a salvage yard or a parts store and asking for a suspension system. You must first ask yourself some questions about your dune buggy to determine precisely the kind of suspension you'll need for your individual application.

How are you planning to use your dune buggy? If you want to do a lot of off-road driving on rocky, rugged trails, then you will want a heavy-duty off-road or racing suspension. On the other hand, if you plan to show your dune buggy in contests, you might want to consider a new aluminum suspension. However, if your plans for the buggy are more along the lines of moderate off-road driving, a good used suspension should work quite well.

What is your budget for a front suspension? Buying a completely new suspension could run as little as $350 to $500, but it could also cost $1,000 or more, which may be beyond your budget. Yet finding a used unit at a salvage yard could wind up costing more than you think, if you end up replacing parts or sections of the suspension.

Here's an example of a good, used ball joint front suspension. On first look, it appears that all pieces are intact.

After closer inspection, though, spots of rust were found on the used unit.

Spotty rust can be fixed, as shown here, with a piece of custom-cut steel that can be welded in place to cover the rust and restore its structural integrity.

How quickly do you need your suspension installed? If you need a suspension right away, rebuilt stock units from your local parts outlet will be the fastest way. By purchasing a completely rebuilt stock unit, all you need to do is paint it the desired color and bolt it in place.

If you have more time, searching for a good used suspension can be rewarding — both economically and emotionally. A used suspension can be found at a salvage yard or an auto swap meet, especially a VW meet. The units found at a swap meet offer a couple of advantages. First, these units were probably taken from a VW Bug, meaning you won't have to make a lot of changes. Second, seeing a used suspension already off the vehicle allows for greater visual inspection. Prices for used suspensions in good condition start at about $50, which would be considerably less than a rebuild. This monetary savings, along with the "thrill of the hunt," makes searching for a used suspension a fun part of building your buggy.

If you have rust that has eaten all the way through a part of the suspension unit, do yourself a favor and look for a better one. Severe rust like this can cause structural damage.

Once you have answered these questions, you must choose the right type of suspension. All have their advantages, so you will need to decide which is the best for your situation.

King pin front suspensions were used on VW Bugs through 1965, and can still be found in good or rebuilt condition. Some rebuilt king pin

Two rebuilt stock units, painted and ready to bolt on your buggy, are shown here. The suspension at the top is a king-pin type, while the bottom unit is a ball-joint type. Lowering kits (right) are available for these units and they can be purchased assembled with the units or you can purchase them separately and install them yourself, but only with the proper equipment and skills.

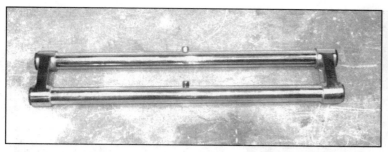

Here's a shiny, new aluminum front suspension, good for light off-roading and for show. All it needs now are torsion bars, torsion seals, torsion arms, king pin units and spindles.

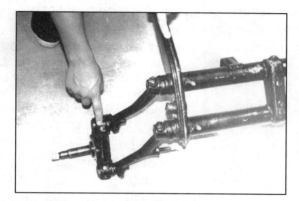

This is a king pin type front suspension. Notice that there are no ball joints, and the shock towers are shaped differently than those used with a ball-joint suspension.

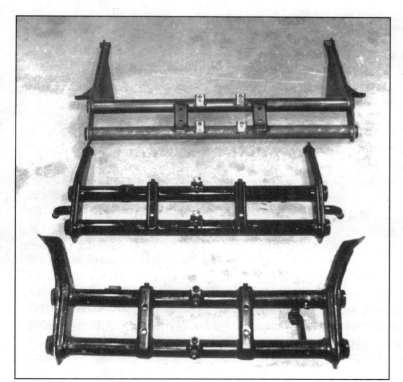

Alignment on a ball-joint suspension is achieved thru adjustment of the tie rods and this adjustment cam. This is something that's best left to the pros at the alignment shop as specialized equipment is required.

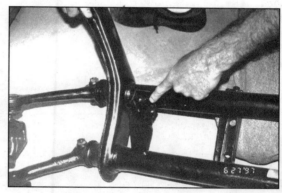

If you purchase a stock rebuilt unit or a used one in good condition, you will need to remove the factory-welded steering gear stop in order to install the unit on your dune buggy. After it is installed, fabricate a new steering gear stop to keep your front tires from hitting the frame or body.

The top unit in this photo is for racing and heavy off-roading. Notice that the beam is wider than the stock units shown below it.

units have adjustable torsion for raising or lowering the front of the vehicle. This is a nice option to have, as you can easily match the front height of your buggy to the terrain. If you don't purchase a suspension with installed height adjusters, there are weld-in adjusters available. These will require that you cut your suspension tubes one at a time. Installing these adjusters should preferably be done by someone experienced in this procedure, although instructions are available from most dune buggy shops for those who are qualified.

If building a light weight buggy for sand-dune hopping is your goal, or if you plan to enter your buggy in show competition, you will want to consider an aluminum suspension. These lightweight, streamlined polished units are predominantly used for operating in sand dunes, moderate trail riding and on show buggies. They can also be used with or without shock towers. Yet there are limitations to this type of suspension. Aluminum units come only in king pin-type models and it is necessary to install torsion bars, torsion seals, torsion arms, king pin units and spindles. You can tackle this task yourself, or some shops can pre-assemble these units for an additional fee.

Those interested in serious off-road driving over very rough roads, or wanting to race their buggy, will need to search for a racing suspension. The beam width on this type of suspension is six inches wider than a normal stock suspension to allow for added stability in hard turns, high speeds and uneven terrain. The height of the shock towers will also be taller than that of a stock unit to compensate for harder landings. Lengthened shock towers are available as an aftermarket part if you want to cut your old king pin shock towers off and add these units to non-racing suspensions.

STREET/MODERATE OFF ROAD

If this is your goal, then a good used unit will work quite well. A salvage yard could possibly have your front suspension. That was the first

The shock tower for a racing suspension is taller than normal to allow the shock absorber greater travel room on hard landings and uneven terrain.

place I visited when searching for a front suspension.

Be sure to inspect used units very carefully because after sitting in a wrecking yard they have a tendency to rust badly in critical areas.

If you find one with rust in such vital areas, do yourself a favor and look for a better one. Repairing this type of damage can be done by welding a tower repair kit to the existing towers, but keep in mind that severe rust in these areas causes structural weakness.

REBUILT STOCK UNITS

If your budget permits, this is the hot tip ... purchasing a completely rebuilt stock unit. It's a simple matter of painting the unit to your choice of color or colors and bolting the unit in place. It can't get much easier than that.

If you purchase a stock rebuilt unit or find a good used stock front suspension, you will need to remove the factory welded-on steering gear stop in order to install this unit on a dune buggy.

After it is installed on your dune buggy, fabricate a steering gear stop to prevent your front tires from hitting the buggy frame or body. A king pin front suspension does not incorporate the same type of steering gear stop.

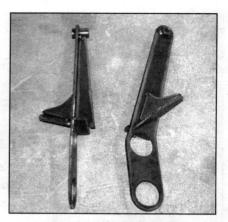

These are the shock towers for the racing suspension with the extra gussets installed for added strength.

Alignment on a ball-joint suspension is performed by adjusting the tie rods and the adjustment cam. Have this done at an alignment shop.

Accompanying photos show the two stock units, the ball joint type and the king pin type.

You can also purchase the front I-beam section separately, but as noted earlier, it will require the installation of torsion bars, I-beam seals, torsion arms, ball joints and spindles. They can also be purchased with or without height adjusters.

OFF ROAD AND RACE SUSPENSION

The beam width on this off road unit is six inches wider than a normal stock unit, to improve stability in hard turns, at high speeds, and on uneven terrain. Also, the height of the shock towers is almost twice that of a stock unit for the express purpose of extra travel with the shock itself to compensate for the harder landings when off roading or racing.

This lengthened shock tower unit is available if you want to cut your old king pin shock towers off and add these units for extra height and strength for use in severe off-road operation. Extra gussets were added for strength.

The gussets would be welded onto the king pin suspension. They

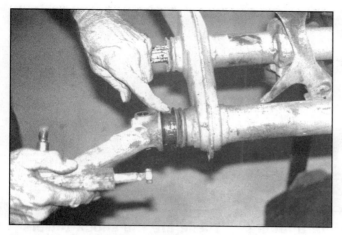

Before installing this good used unit, I decided to replace the dried, cracked torsion arm seals.

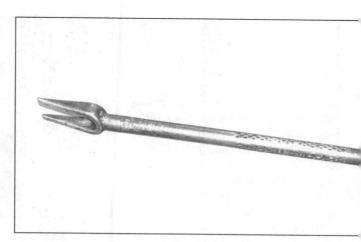

Removal of the spindle from the ball joint was realized by using a "pickle fork."

With the spindle out of the way, loosen the torsion arm lock nut and use an Allen wrench to back the locking stud out far enough to release the tension on the torsion arm.

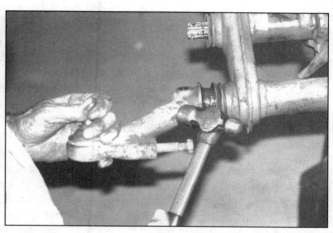

Use a hammer to tap the torsion arm off the torsion bar.

would be welded into place with beefed-up spindle and front torsion arms. The front suspension of a dune buggy is just one more area where you are limited only by the limits of your imagination.

On our project dune buggy I located a good used front suspension that was complete and upon closer inspection appeared to be almost new with minimal wear. Before cleaning and painting the front suspension, I decided to replace all four torsion arm seals, which had become dried out and cracked from age. To replace these seals required the purchase of new seals to fit the unit. If you know the year of the VW Bug

from which the suspension came, it helps in locating the parts. Basically there are two types of torsion seals, either king pin or ball joint. To install the seals the spindle must be removed. Do this by loosening but not completely removing both ball joint retaining nuts. Next, take a tool referred to as a pickle fork and install it between the ball joint and the spindle, then use a hammer to drive the pickle fork inward until the spindle separates from the ball joint. NOTE: Wear eye protection at all times.

Carefully remove the ball joint nut. CAUTION: There is spring tension on the torsion arms and they will spring upward when this nut is

removed. After the spindle is out of the way, loosen the torsion arm lock nut; then, using an Allen wrench, back the locking stud out far enough to release the tension for the removal of the torsion arm. Next, use a hammer and tap the torsion arm off the torsion bar. Now that you have access to the defective seals, take a chisel or similar tool and, with a hammer, gently tap out the old seals. After cleaning the seal area, install the new seal. It might require gentle tapping to seat. Follow the same procedure on the remaining replacement seal. With both new seals in place, reverse the above procedure to reinstall the torsion arms and the spindle. Having

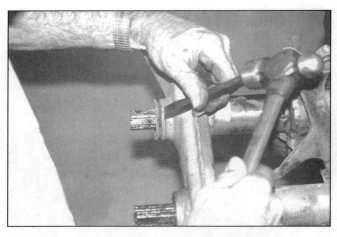

After loosening the torsion arm, remove the arm by pulling it toward you while gently rocking it back and forth.

Using a chisel, remove the dried out seals. Clean the seal area, then install the new seal. This might require a gentle tapping to get the seal in place.

To install the new seals, insert them into the housing groove and push them forward. They also may require gentle tapping to properly seat.

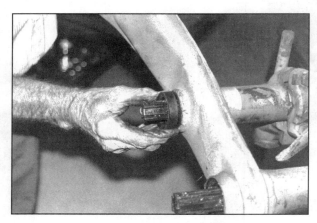

completed one side of the front suspension, move over to the opposite side and repeat the same procedure. Now that the seals have been replaced a thorough cleaning, sanding and painting is in order. When completely dried, the like new front suspension can be installed; be sure to use grade five or stronger bolts. ■

Once the new seals have been installed and the torsion arms and spindles have been reinstalled, give the suspension a complete cleaning and painting. Here, Randy Hamilton is sanding the suspension in preparation for painting.

Using a power wire brush, Roy Owens removes surface rust from the suspension prior to sanding and painting.

Owens gives the suspension an even coat of glossy black spray paint. CAUTION: A mask is always recommended when painting.

Our front suspension — looking as good as new!

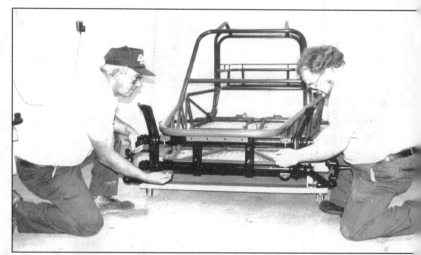

After the unit is completely dry, Roy and Randy carefully bolt it into place.

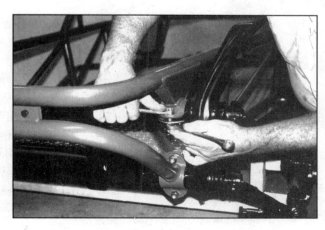

Use grade five or stronger bolts to secure the suspension to the buggy.

Installing the Steering Gear Box, Tie Rods and Steering Shaft

Pointing You in the Right Direction

Steering is the most critical system on a dune buggy from a safety standpoint, along with brakes and tires, so don't cut any corners here. Use only quality new, rebuilt or used components and make extra sure they're properly installed.

The steering gearbox used on the project buggy was a used unit salvaged from a 1973 VW bug, which performed up to specs in road testing prior to removal of the unit. NOTE: We used a gearbox from a VW Bug I-beam suspension on the project buggy. The gearbox from a VW Super Beetle will not work because a Super Beetle front suspension is a McPherson strut system, therefore requiring a different type of gearbox.

First, we gave the used gearbox a good cleaning with a strong solvent and then we squirted it with aluminum paint. With the front suspension

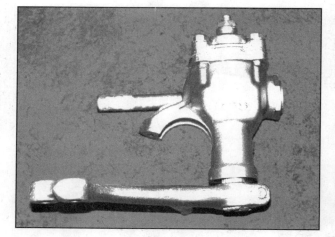

After a good cleaning with an industrial-strength solvent, the used steering gearbox was spray painted in an aluminum finish. It looked great.

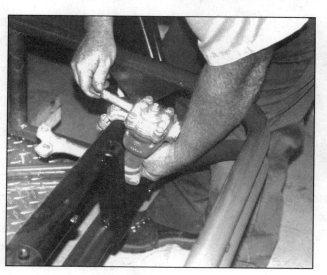

With the front suspension bolted in place it was time to install the steering gearbox. We started by holding the gearbox in position over the gearbox alignment pin that is welded onto the front suspension. Then we started the retaining bolts by hand.

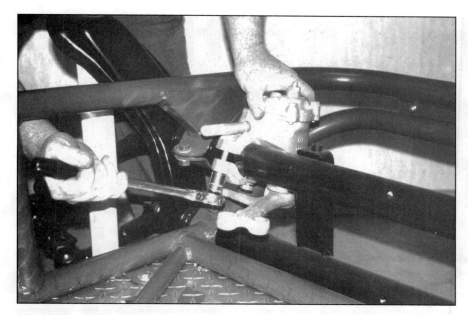

We then tightened the retaining bolts with a socket and ratchet.

After cleaning both steering couplers, the next order of business was to install the used gearbox coupler and steering shaft coupler.

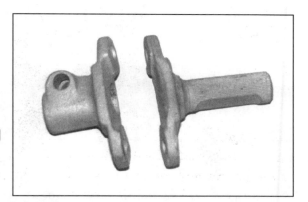

We first installed the gearbox coupler onto the shaft that sticks out of the gearbox.

securely bolted into place, we installed the steering gearbox. To be properly installed, the gearbox must be positioned over the gearbox alignment pin welded onto the front suspension.

After cleaning both steering couplers, the gearbox coupler and the steering shaft coupler, we installed them. First, we installed the gearbox coupler onto the shaft that sticks out of the gearbox. This coupler can only be installed one way if it is to work properly, so make sure you install it correctly. When correctly mounted, the bolt will go through the steering coupler and the slot in the steering shaft. It must also be tightened securely.

We considered disassembling two used front tie rods, both the right and left sides, cleaning and painting the tie rods themselves, then installing new inner and outer tie rod ends. This would have worked great but, by the time we finished pricing the parts and considering the extra labor involved to disassemble, clean, paint and reassemble everything, it was more cost efficient to buy new tie rods completely assembled and ready to install. All we had to do was paint them. After they dried, we installed the tie rod assemblies, as demonstrated in the accompanying photos and captions.

NOTE: Final adjustments to both tie rods will be performed when the project buggy goes to the alignment shop to have the front end aligned.

At this point, we installed a new steering damper. A damper is a must because it absorbs the shock and vibration caused by the tires and suspension contacting bumps or potholes. Without it the front tires can shake after hitting a bump, causing violent movement of the steering wheel. There's no way to analyze the condition of a used damper, so always use a new one.

To install the steering shaft required a new steering coupler (never re-use a used one). Our steering shaft consisted of two pieces, the shaft itself and the steering shaft bearing. The shaft can be purchased

We then inserted a new bolt through the coupler.

Then, after installing a new lock washer and nut on the bolt, we tightened them securely with two wrenches

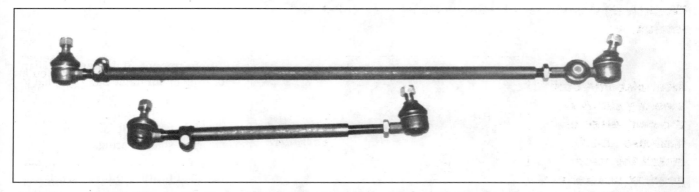

After considering the use of used units, and pricing everything, we elected to simply purchase new tie rods with tie rod ends. The new units were completely assembled and ready to go, except they needed to be painted. We painted ours black.

With the paint dry on our new tie rods, we installed the left outer tie rod first. This was done by inserting the tapered shaft of the tie rod end into the tapered hole of the left outer spindle (above, left). NOTE: It really doesn't matter which side goes on first. We then installed a locking nut and tightened it securely (above, right). Remember, it must be tight.

We then installed
the tapered shaft
of the left inner tie
rod end into the
steering box
Pitman shaft arm.
Next, we installed
a new locking nut
and tightened it
securely.

either chrome plated or in raw steel to be painted in any color you want.

Then we installed the shaft. First, we measured the desired length of the shaft to fit our particular buggy frame so that the steering wheel ends up in the proper location for the driver. It has to be custom-fitted to each buggy application. Second, after cutting the steering shaft to the desired length, we inserted the steering shaft coupler into the hollow shaft, again making sure that the steering bearing has been installed on the shaft prior to this. Next, have the coupler professionally welded to the shaft. A professional weld is imperative. After assembling our steering shaft, we installed the new steering coupler and connected the steering shaft to the gearbox.

To mount the steering shaft bearing to our frame bar, I decided to bolt a length of angle metal to the lower window frame bar and then drill two holes in it for mounting the steering shaft bearing. It was then simply a matter of bolting the steering shaft bearing to the bracket.

That completed the installation of the steering box, tie rods and steering shaft. ∎

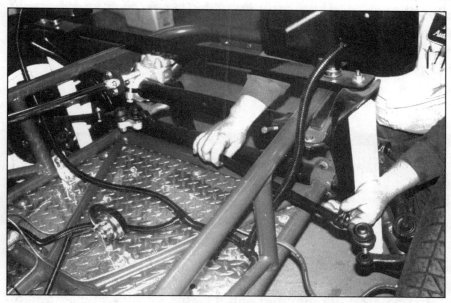

We then went to the right side of the buggy and installed the right tie rod in the same order as the left side.

Once again, we inserted the tapered ends into their respective holes, both on the outer tie rod end and the inner tie rod end that connects to the gearbox.

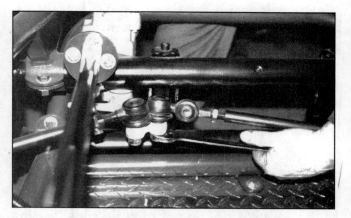

Using lock nuts, we secured the assembly. We torqued everything down tight. NOTE: Final adjustments to both of the tie rods will be made at the time we take the project buggy to the alignment shop to have the front end aligned.

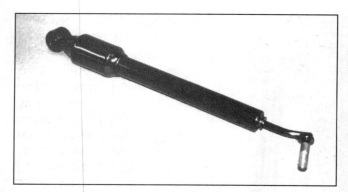

A brand new steering damper was purchased at an off-road shop. NOTE: This little device is a must. Its purpose is to absorb the shock and vibration caused by the tires and suspension coming into contact with rough roads or bumps. Without it the front tires can shake after hitting a bump, causing violent movement of the steering wheel.

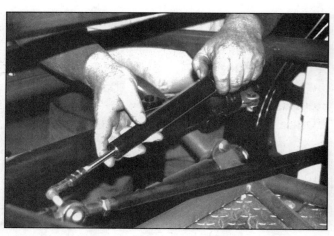

With both tie rods on and secured, we proceeded to install the new steering damper.

We then inserted the threaded rod end into the right inner tie rod end mounting hole located near the gearbox.

We then installed a lock nut on the threaded end near the gearbox and tightened it securely.

Next, we inserted a new bolt through the mounting hole at the other end of the damper.

Then we tightened the damper securely to the bracket.

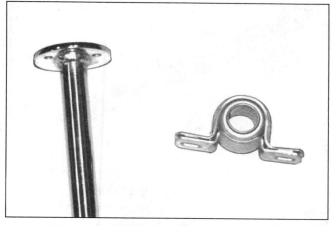

To install our steering shaft, we needed a new steering coupler. Never install a used one because there's no way to tell its condition due to age, wear and damage.

Our steering shaft consists of two pieces. The first is the shaft itself (left), which can be purchased either in raw steel (to be painted in the color of your choice), or chrome plated. The second piece is the steering shaft bearing (right).

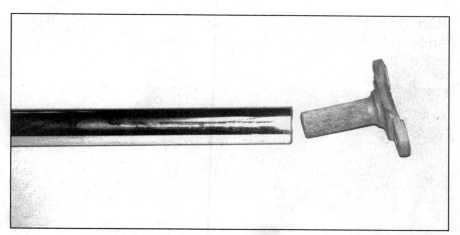

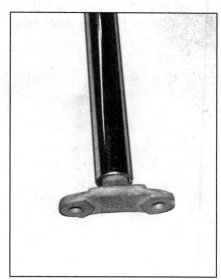

To start the steering shaft assembly, the top priority is to install the bearing onto the shaft first.

Then on the other end of the steering shaft two things must be done. First, measure the desired length of the shaft to fit your particular buggy frame so that the steering wheel ends up in the proper location for the driver. Second, after cutting the steering shaft to the desired length (above), insert the steering shaft coupler into the hollow shaft (left).

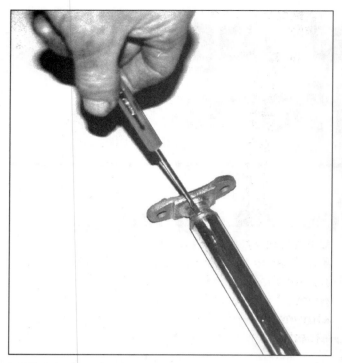

After we had finished the assembly of our steering shaft, we installed the new steering coupler and connected the steering shaft to the gearbox. Always follow the installation instructions supplied with the new steering coupler.

With this done, we had the coupler professionally welded to the shaft, as seen in this photo.

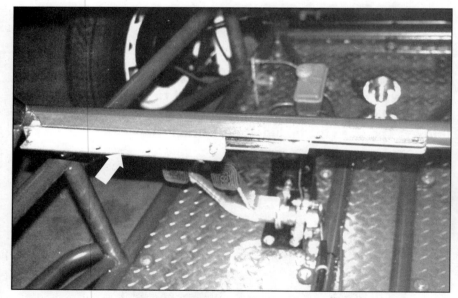

It was then a simple matter of bolting the steering shaft bearing to the bracket.

To mount the steering shaft bearing to our frame bar, we opted to bolt a length of angle metal to the lower window frame bar and then drill two holes in it for mounting the steering shaft bearing (arrow).

Installing the Horn

Beep! Beep! Move Over Road Runner!

To keep varmints out of your way, warn other motorists of your intentions and keep everyone alert, a horn is more of a necessity than an option on any street-driven buggy, and is even recommended on dune buggies operated exclusively off road (makes a good distress signal).

The horn we chose is a universal 12-volt horn that is available at most auto part stores. We elected to locate the horn on the floor pan toward the front of the dune buggy where it would be nice and audible, yet out of the way.

The horn came in a kit complete with an L-bracket and mounting hardware, although we added a lock washer. It comes ready to install.

First, we marked the location on the floor pan for the hole, then drilled a 5/16-inch hole at that point. We then bolted the bracket to the floor using the 5/16-inch bolt and nut provided in the horn kit, adding the lock washer for extra insurance against it vibrating loose. Then we inserted the mounting stud on the horn through a second hole in the horn bracket and installed the nut and washer. It was that simple.

All it needs now is to be hooked up, which is described in detail in the wiring section of this manual. ∎

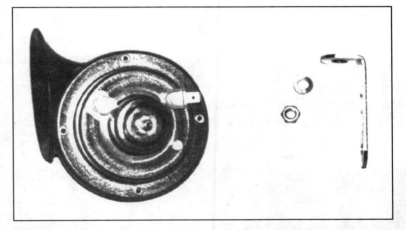

After selecting your horn, you need to determine where you want to mount it. I decided to locate my horn on the floor pan toward the front of the dune buggy. The horn kit included an L-bracket.

We marked the location on the floor pan for drilling the single mounting hole.

Next we drilled a 5/16-inch hole through the floor pan.

After that, we bolted the bracket to the floor with a 5/16-inch bolt with nut and lock washer, tightening it down with a closed-end wrench.

Then we inserted the mounting stud on the horn through the remaining hole in the horn bracket and installed the nut and washer.

Using a wrench, we secured the horn to the bracket. That's it; it's installed, ready to be wired.

Selecting and Installing the Brakes

More Power! More Stopping Power, that is!

The braking system is one of the most important features of any dune buggy. Once you're in motion, it's the only way you're going to stop, other than hitting something, and that could happen right now with malfunctioning or inadequate brakes. So exercise extreme care in selecting and installing the all-important brake system.

The variety of brake systems and options available is expansive. In my many years of being involved with buggy builders and going to buggy shows, I have seen numerous examples of state-of-the-art braking systems. These systems include such items as street legal disc brake kits for front and rear suspensions. These include new brake calipers and mounting hardware designed to adapt to stock VW Bug front and rear suspensions, and do it as bolt-on units. The rear disc brake kits can also be purchased with emergency brake capabilities built in. Then you can add braided front and rear stainless steel brake hoses, semi-metallic disc brake pads, stainless steel brake lines, and super Hi-tech hydraulic master cylinder or cylinders that provide the fluid pressure adequate to operate all of these components.

I've also seen braking systems

By scouting local VW bug swap meets, we located two good used front brake backing plates, one used rear backing plate, and one new rear backing plate. The function of these units is to hold all the necessary brake parts, such as wheel cylinders, brake shoes, retaining pins, and the emergency brake cables on the rear brake system.

After carefully inspecting the backing plates, we thoroughly cleaned them using a strong solvent. Then we painted them with black semi-gloss enamel.

We started the installation process by mounting one of the rear backing plates on our previously installed rear torsion arm.

After installing the rear backing plate, we installed the backing plate retaining cap. This cap holds the backing plate in place.

With the backing plate retaining cap in place, we installed the previously saved and cleaned cap bolts and torqued them to factory specifications.

After installing the backing plate and retaining cap, we proceeded with the installation of our new wheel cylinder.

that only marginally work, due to worn or leaking parts, such as rusted brake lines or blown wheel cylinders, improper installation, and even gross neglect. The result is an unsafe vehicle. Any money you spend to install a high quality, efficient brake system will be money well spent.

On the project dune buggy, I elected to use a stock VW Bug brake system, with either new, rebuilt, or reconditioned used parts. CAUTION: Do not cut corners on any part of your brake system. If a part is even mildly suspect, don't use it.

I also chose a dual master cylinder because of the extra measure of safety it provides. A dual master

cylinder has a separate section for the front brakes and a separate section for the rear brakes. I have incorporated the dual master cylinder setup on every dune buggy I've built. I also installed a manually operated emergency brake for the rear brakes as a backup.

We started the brake installation on the rear of the buggy, and then went to the front. After we had completed one side, we went to the other side and performed the same procedure. We started by installing the backing plates. The function of these units is to hold all of the necessary brake parts, such as the wheel cylinders, brake shoes, and retaining pins,

plus the emergency brake cables on the rear brake system. CAUTION: If you decide to install used backing plates, they must be carefully inspected for worn areas, especially where the brake shoes rub. They must also be checked for rust. If you find any serious rust or badly worn places, DO NOT USE THEM.

When installing the rear brake backing plate, the hole for the wheel cylinder must be at the top, or in the up position, and the brake adjusters must be at the bottom of the backing plate. To secure the backing plate to the torsion arm, we installed the retaining cap. This retaining cap must have a new seal installed in it

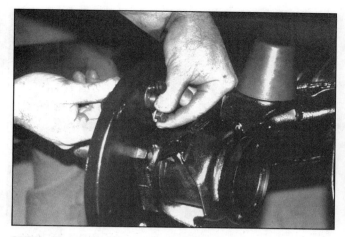

With the wheel cylinder in place and fitted flush with the backing plate, it was time to install the wheel cylinder retaining bolt. (You can use the saved original bolt or a new replacement bolt.)

With the bolt installed and tight, we then lubricated all brake shoe rub points, and the cavity where the brake adjusters reside.

Be sure to adequately lubricate the brake adjusters.

With the wheel cylinder installed and both brake adjusters in place, the backing plate looked like this. Also note the previously installed spacer (arrow), which slips over the rear spindle to provide

a smooth surface for the seal in the backing plate retaining cap. It is very important that you do not forget this spacer.

before mounting it to the torsion arm. The purpose of this seal is to keep dirt and water out of your rear spindle bearings. There is also a spacer that slides over the spindle on which this seal rides.

Next we installed the four retaining bolts and tightened them to specs. These torque specs will vary depending upon the year and type of rear torsion arms you are using. After tightening all four bolts, we checked to make sure the rear spindle still turned freely with no excessive friction.

Then came the wheel cylinder

installation. I highly recommend new wheel cylinders because used wheel cylinders that have been subjected to sitting outside in a wrecking yard for extended periods, possibly many years, have a tendency to rust both externally and internally. When they rust internally, it causes pitting of the bore surface, which makes them susceptible to leakage, thereby rendering them very unsafe to use.

With all rear brake parts installed per the procedures detailed in the accompanying photos and captions, we then went over our rear brake checklist before installing the brake drum:

• Are all the brake springs, pins and retainers in place and secured properly?

• Are all wheel cylinders and backing plate bolts torqued to specs?

• Are brake adjusting slots aligned properly?

• Is the spindle spacer for the retaining cap seal installed on the spindle?

• Has the rear brake drum been cleaned, inspected and resurfaced if necessary?

• Is the emergency brake cable properly installed and secured?

After the rear drum was on and

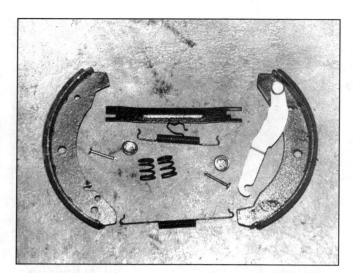

This is a typical rear brake shoe and brake spring kit.

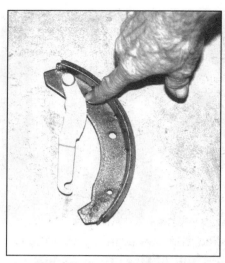

We are now ready to assemble the rear brakes and springs, with the emergency brake levers. The two emergency brake levers are different by design; there is one for the left side and one for the right side, and they will not interchange.

the spindle nut had been torqued to specs, we installed a new cotter pin through the slot in the spindle and the spindle nut to keep this nut secure. This now completed the rear brake drum assembly, except for adjustments and the bleeding of the rear brakes, which we will perform later.

We then moved on to installing the front brakes. The front brake backing plates differ from the rear in that there are no retaining caps to install, or emergency brake cables to hook up. By following the photos and captions for installing the front brakes, and before putting the front drum on, we went over this checklist:

- Are all front brake retaining pins and springs in place and properly secured?

- Have all rub points been lubricated? NOTE: Never put oil or grease on any brake linings, either front or rear.

- Are all adjustment slots properly lined up?

- Are all wheel cylinder and backing plate retaining bolts in place and properly torqued to factory specifications?

- Has the front brake drum been cleaned, inspected, and resurfaced if necessary, and have both the inner and outer wheel bearings

With the levers and springs assembled, as shown here, we carefully slid the unit into place by slanting it upward, and guiding the

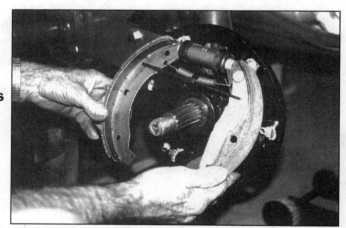

tabs on the upper part of the brake shoes into the slots of the wheel cylinder pistons.

Now, with the new hold down pins, we secured the brake assembly to the backing plate.

Then we installed the remaining new brake spring at the bottom of the brake shoes.

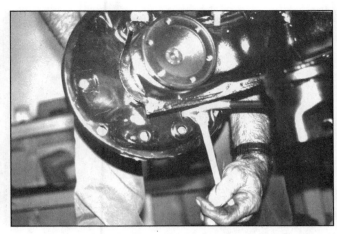

Next, we installed the emergency cable by inserting it through the rear of the backing plate and securing it with the cable retaining clip and bolt.

With the cable securely in place, we hooked the cable to the rear brake lever.

With everything checked and rechecked as per our checklist (outlined in the text), we were now ready to install the rear brake drum on the spindle.

been properly lubricated and fitted with new front drum grease seals?

The front dust cover was the next item to install. The typical VW Bug ball joint front suspension requires a separate front bearing dust cover for the left front, and the right front. The reason for this is that the left front wheel bearing dust cover has a stamped square slot in it for the installation of the speedometer cable. The cable comes through the back side of the left front spindle, travels through the center of the spindle, and installs in the square slot in the dust cover cap.

You should now have your front and rear brakes assembled and secured on the one side of your dune buggy. Now proceed to the other side and follow the same steps and complete that side to this point.

Assuming that you have both front and rear brake drum assemblies completed, it is now time to proceed with the emergency brake handle assembly. The emergency brake system consists of two new emergency brake cables, one emergency brake handle, one rubber boot, an emergency brake cable routing unit, mounting braces, and attaching bolts. It was necessary to manufacture brackets for the emergency brake

lever. After the pieces were bent by inserting them in a bench vise and bending them by hand into the proper shape, we drilled 3/8-inch holes into the outer portion of the bottom legs. We then mounted our braces to the floor pan. Then we marked and drilled our braces to accept the cable guide and handle unit.

After the exact length of the cables had been calculated, we cut the excess off the emergency brake cables. This is a tough chore as the cables are very strong, but it can be accomplished with a good set of side cutters. We then inserted the cables into the cable shortening kits and

After installing the rear brake drum, we screwed the large nut on the spindle.

We then torqued the nut to factory specifications. NOTE: Proper torquing of this nut is critical.

We started the front brakes by first installing the backing plate to the spindle. Note the location of the hole in the backing plate for the wheel cylinder (arrow). This hole should be pointing to the rear of the dune buggy, with the brake adjusting wheels pointing toward the front.

With the backing plate in place we installed the previously saved retaining bolts, and secured the backing plate to the spindle, then torqued to factory specifications.

secured them with the locking screws. We could now install both emergency brake cables to the emergency brake handle unit and temporarily install the adjusting nuts, but we did not make any final adjustments at this time. The final adjustments will be made after all the brakes have been adjusted and the complete brake system has had all the air purged from the hydraulic part of the system. This procedure is commonly referred to as bleeding the brakes.

When we had completed the installation of all four-wheel brake assemblies and the emergency brake system, we could then install the dual brake master cylinder, but to accomplish this, we must first install a master cylinder and pedal assembly bracket on the floor pan. NOTE: There are numerous types of these brackets available, I have always used the 3/16-inch thick steel bracket. This particular bracket is very sturdy and is definitely worthwhile in terms of both durability and safety.

Before drilling mounting holes through the bracket and the floor pan, the exact location of this bracket must be determined. This can be calculated by temporarily placing your dune buggy seat on the floor pan in its proper location. It will not be necessary to bolt the seat to the floor pan at this time. We then had an assistant sit in the driver's seat and assume a comfortable position. Then we marked the location for the pedal bracket and master cylinder, drilled mounting holes, secured the bracket

Then we positioned the wheel cylinder on the backing plate, making sure it was flush with the backing plate.

We now installed the wheel cylinder retaining bolt and torqued to factory specs.

to the floor pan, and installed the master cylinder.

Now we fabricated two brackets that were used to hold our two front rubber brake hoses securely to the floor pan. Here again this was a simple task achieved by cutting two pieces of 1-1/2 x 1/8 aluminum stock at five inches in length and making one 90 degree angle bend at three inches and then drilling one 5/8-inch hole in the longer end to hold the female end of the rubber brake hose. We then drilled two 5/16-inch holes in the shorter end of each bracket. Before making the 90 degree angle bend in the bracket, be aware that the end with the larger hole must be up high enough to adequately clear the height of the lower frame bar.

With the project dune buggy's front suspension being a stock VW bug ball joint type, 19-inch VW bug brake hoses worked perfectly. I have found that this particular length of rubber brake hose has fit all the dune buggies I have built. On your project buggy, check for proper length and clearance, make sure they are long enough to allow a full and normal front wheel turning radius but that they are not excessively long, which could cause rubbing and kinking.

CAUTION: On your project buggy, this clearance must be checked with your wheels and tires installed and the front wheels turned fully to the right and then fully to the left.

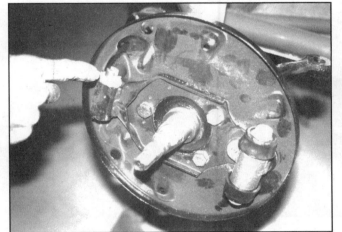

After lubricating and installing the brake adjusters, we lubricated all brake shoe rub points just as we did on the rear brakes.

A typical front brake shoe and spring kit will look like this.

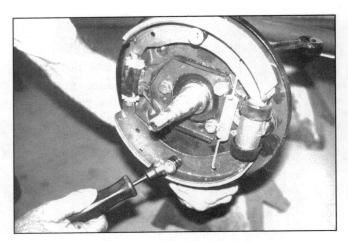

We installed the new front brakes with new front brake springs in this fashion, making sure all clips and springs were secured properly. NOTE: Make sure all adjusting slots line up precisely, and that the brake shoes are installed in the slots of the wheel-cylinder pistons. Also, brake shoes will insert into the adjusters only one way for a correct installation, and that's with the lower part of the angle in the adjustor's slot pointing inward toward the spindle. It's the same for the rear brakes.

A completed front brake installation should appear like this. Before proceeding, refer to the front brake checklist (in the text).

Now that we have all four brake drums on and tight, our master cylinder was then bolted securely in place. With all the rubber brake hoses in their respective wheel cylinders and mounting brackets, we were now ready to install the remainder of our metal brake lines. By using both front and rear suspensions from a parted out 1973 VW Bug, we were able to purchase a complete brake line kit that was an original equipment type for that year and model VW. Replacement metal brake lines come in straight lengths that require bending and forming, which is normally a simple task because the metal is soft and easily bent. Care must be taken not to kink the line when making a tight bend, though.

When measuring for exact lengths of metal brake lines for your dune buggy frame, do not measure too short. If a line is slightly too long, it can be bent to fit well and look good, but a line that is too short simply will not work. Measure for your brake lines at least 1 to 2 inches longer than needed.

After proper metal brake line lengths were measured and purchased, we started by installing the longest line, which is the one running from the rear of the master cylinder to the left rear brake T-fitting, then we installed the remaining lines. We were now very close to having a new and workable brake system. Installing the brake fluid reservoir was next. The new brake fluid reservoir can be mounted in any number of areas, but it is very simple to form a bracket out of aluminum stock to hold the reservoir approximately five inches above the master cylinder. We fabricated a mounting bracket out of aluminum stock to handle this.

Now that all brake components were on and secure, we began the bleeding process. We filled the master cylinder reservoir and started with the right rear wheel cylinder and began bleeding the brakes. To bleed the brakes, an assistant pumps the brakes until resistance is felt and then the bleeder screw is slowly opened to remove the air that was trapped in the system. By continuing

this pumping and bleeding process enough times, eventually we produced an even flow of brake fluid that contained no air bubbles.

Then we moved to the left rear wheel cylinder and performed the same procedure.

CAUTION: Continually check the master cylinder reservoir to avoid pumping it empty of brake fluid. If you pump it empty, air will get back into the system and it will be necessary to start the bleeding process all over again.

With both rear wheel cylinders bled and free of air, we proceeded to the right front and performed the same pump, hold and bleed procedure. Finally we went to the left front wheel cylinder and performed what will hopefully be our final pump, hold and bleed procedure. Most older brake systems are bled in the order we just used, which is right rear, left rear, right front, left front.

Now that all the air was out of the hydraulic brake system, and we had a reasonably solid brake pedal, we adjusted all four brakes, using this procedure on each wheel. NOTE: There are two brake adjusters on each wheel; on the rear wheels there are front and rear shoe adjusters, on the front wheels there are top and bottom shoe adjusters.

We adjusted the first of the two-brake shoe adjusters until we felt a

heavy drag on the brake drum while turning the drum in a forward direction. We then backed off the adjuster until a slight drag was felt. We then did the same thing to the other adjuster. By performing this adjustment on all four wheels our brake pedal proved to be very solid, and traveled approximately two to three inches from its stationary position before engagement of the brake linings to the drum.

We then tightened the adjustment nuts on both emergency brake cables, until pulling up on the emergency brake lever three to four inches from its parked position held the rear brake drums securely.

CAUTION: Should you feel a soft pedal or the pedal goes almost to the floor the first time you pump it, this is an indication that either air is in the system, or the brakes are badly out of adjustment. Before you call the brake system finished, recheck all connections and fittings for leaks, and after the initial road test, check the entire brake system again, including master cylinder, wheel cylinders, brakes lines, connections, etc.

It's one thing if your dune buggy won't go, but it's something else — and a lot more dangerous and scary — if it won't stop! ∎

Everything checked out fine, so we installed the front brake drum.

After the drum was on the spindle, we made sure it was turning freely with no adverse friction. We then installed the outer front wheel bearing and the notched bearing washer.

Then we secured the assembly with a special lock nut (left). To tighten the front wheel bearing lock nuts, follow the factory recommendations to the letter, because if they're either too loose or too tight, severe wheel bearing damage and even failure can occur. After tightening to factory specs, we locked the outer bearing nut in place with the locking screw that's built into the special nut (middle). We then installed the outer wheel bearing dust cover by gently tapping it into place with a hammer (right).

NOTE: This is a pressed fit which might require more than a gentle tap, so watch your fingers. With this finished we set our sights on the emergency brake system.

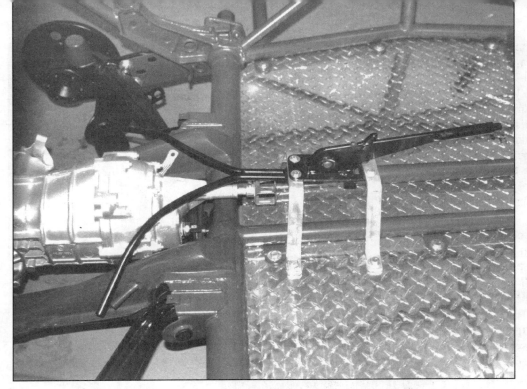

It was necessary to manufacture the mounting braces, which actually turned out to be rather routine. It required two pieces of one inch by 1/8-inch aluminum stock cut to an overall length of 16 inches and then bent to form a bridge as seen here. We then mounted the brake lever unit to the braces.

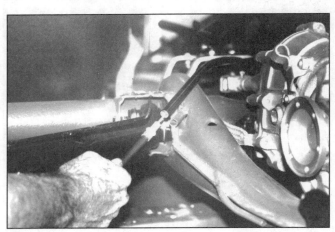

The next step was to take both rear emergency brake cables and insert them through each of the cable guide tubes.

Once both cables had been properly inserted, it was necessary to install a cable shortening kit on each cable. Both cables must be pulled snug but not overly tight with the emergency brake handle in the down position. This must be done before exact cable length can be properly determined.

After the emergency brake was workable, we started the installation of the pedal bracket. First I had the primary driver of the dune buggy sit in the driver's seat and assume a comfortable driving position.

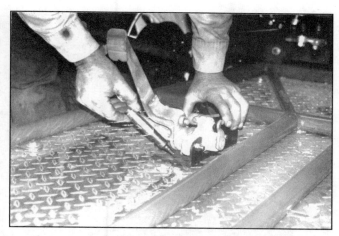

Then I had an assistant temporarily position the pedal assembly bracket on the floor pan where it was at a comfortable length from the driver for proper operation of the clutch, brake and gas pedals.

After this location had been determined, we marked the location on the floor pan.

We then drilled four 3/8-inch holes through the pedal bracket and through the floor pan, making sure to drill one hole in each of the four corners of the bracket for maximum strength.

To secure this bracket to the floor, use industrial strength nuts, bolts, and lock washers.

Once we had secured the pedal bracket to the floor pan, we proceeded with the final installation of the previously painted clutch and brake pedal assembly.

Next, we positioned the dual-brake master cylinder.

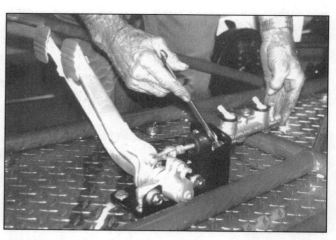

We then secured the master cylinder to the pedal bracket.

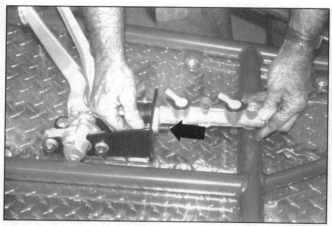

We made sure all bolts were of the proper length and size to fit the master cylinder. Plus, we had one of the master cylinder retaining bolts (arrow) that was at least 1/4-inch longer than normal. This bolt will be used to secure the bracket that will support the dual brake fluid reservoir, hence the needed extra length.

When we had finished the manufacture of the two rubber brake hose brackets, we drilled two 5/16-inch holes in one end as seen here. The smaller holes will be used for the mounting of the bracket to the floor pan.

Then we drilled two 5/16-holes in the floor pan for the hose brackets. We then positioned the brackets approximately parallel with where the front brake hose screws into the front brake wheel cylinder.

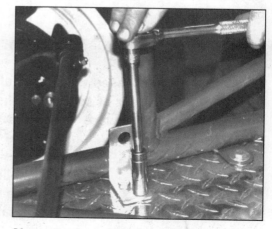

Now we secured the bracket to the floor pan with nuts, bolts and lock washers.

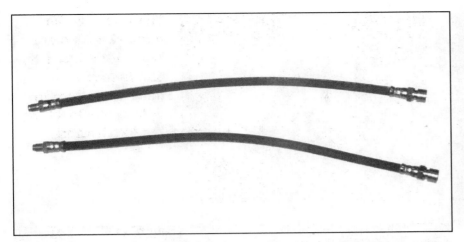

Next on the agenda was the installation of these stock VW brake hoses.

We installed both front rubber brake hoses into the wheel cylinders. The male end goes into the wheel cylinder while the female end is routed through the bracket, as seen here. Turning clockwise, screw the male end in first and tighten it, then insert the female end into the bracket.

With the brackets and hoses in place we secured them with new brake hose clips.

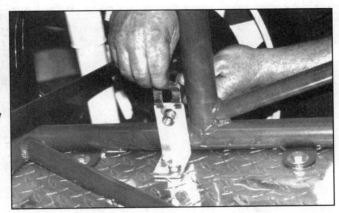

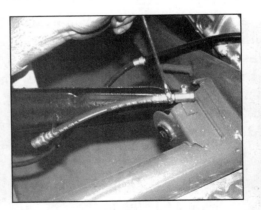

The rubber brake hoses we installed on the rear of the project dune buggy were purchased as original equipment to fit a 1973 VW Bug rear torsion.

It also required one hose splicer which goes on the right side of the rear torsion housing. We screwed the male end of the rubber brake hose into this splicer. With this hose in place, we tightened until properly seated.

On the left side of the torsion we needed what is called a brake T-fitting. The left rear, or driver's side brake hose, screws into the opening of this T-fitting that is closest to the left rear brake drum.

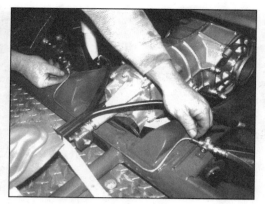

Then we took an original equipment type metal brake line and formed it by hand to fit from the right brake block to the left T-fitting.

After installing this hose and tightening it securely, we placed the female end of both rear rubber brake hoses into the hose brackets, which had been welded onto the original type rear torsion arms, and, using brake hose clips, secured them in place.

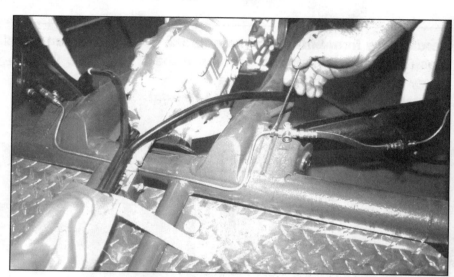

We then tightened this line securely.

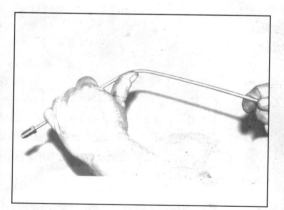

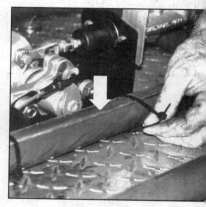

From this point we then installed a new metal brake line from each rear rubber brake hose to each new rear wheel cylinder, and tightened securely.

A slow approach works quite well when forming corners or bends in metal brake lines. NOTE: The curves in all of our brake lines were hand formed using no tools or specialized bending equipment.

With this line (arrow) secured at both ends, we can now either cable strap it, or tie strap it to the buggy frame, or floor pan. We used a combination of ties and straps.

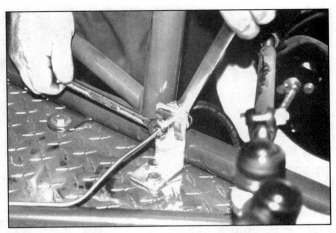

We can now form both front metal brake lines (arrows) to follow the contour of the buggy frame, making sure they avoid any interference with moving parts of the front suspension, or the tires.

We then installed and secured both of these brake lines to their respective brake hoses.

Next, we installed the brake lines at the master cylinder.

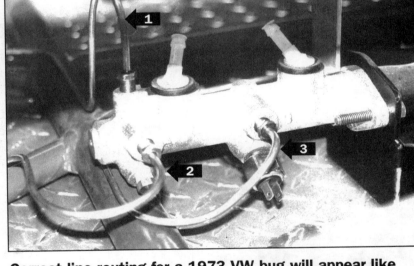

Correct line routing for a 1973 VW bug will appear like this. The proper connections for the right front (1), left front (2) and rear brake (3) lines are indicated by the arrows.

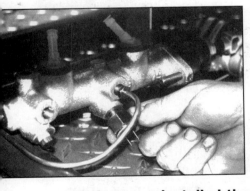

After checking and re-checking all brake line connections, we installed the brake light switch in the master cylinder. NOTE: Most VW Bug dual master cylinders came with two brake light switch ports. You can either block one off with a brake light switch block-off plug, or install both brake light switches and use only one of them for the brake lights.

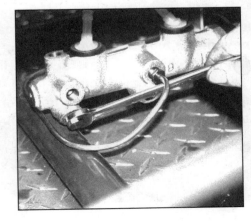

On the project buggy, I decided to block off one switch port as shown here.

We were now very close to having a new and workable brake system. The new brake fluid reservoir can be mounted in any number of areas, but it is very simple to form a bracket

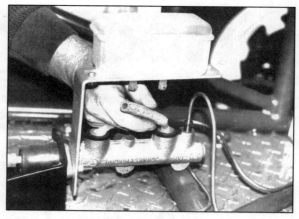

out of aluminum stock to hold the reservoir approximately five inches above the master cylinder. The extra-length bolt that we installed when mounting the master cylinder to the cylinder bracket was now used to mount the reservoir bracket.

After mounting the reservoir to the bracket, we installed a special VW brake fluid hose from the reservoir to the master cylinder. CAUTION: Use only rubber hose that has been manufactured for brake fluid purposes. Fuel line hose will not work.

With everything on and tight we can now fill the reservoir with fresh brake fluid. I then had an assistant slowly pump the brake pedal until resistance was felt. (Sometimes this can take 20-30 pumps.)

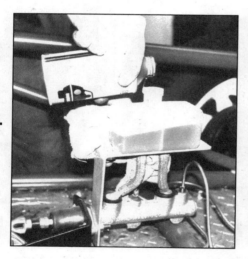

A short length of rubber vacuum hose inserted tightly over the bleeder screw works great for draining the excess brake fluid into a proper container.

After resistance was felt, I had my assistant maintain pressure on the brake pedal while I slowly opened the right rear wheel cylinder bleeder screw. (NOTE: Brake fluid and air will squirt out under pressure. Be sure to wear safety goggles and drain the toxic fluid into a proper container.) After following the bleeding and adjustment procedure outlined in the text, and making a close inspection of all fittings and bolts, a test drive would soon be in order. The project buggy brake system performed perfectly. After the road test, all of the brake system components were visually inspected for leakage.

Hooking Up the Transmission

Getting Power to the Wheels

The transmission is the lifeline link between your engine and the drive wheel or wheels. If it's not going, neither are you. Chose your transmission wisely, keeping in mind such factors as performance, durability, serviceability, etc., as well as cost and availability.

The transmission for our project buggy started out as a used unit. Because we removed it from a 1973 VW Bug that we had driven prior to its removal, we knew that it was in fine working order. You might not have the good fortune of being able to "road test" your transmission before buying it, so here are a few shopping tips that will hopefully help you avoid the aggravation of buying a bad transmission, hauling it home, cleaning it, changing the gear oil, installing it in your buggy, having your buggy ready for its first road test, and then discovering that reverse doesn't work, or that it clangs in one of the other gears. This is a very discouraging situation, and one I know from personal experience. It can be very disheartening, but it can also be avoided in most cases.

If you are looking for a used transmission, try to locate one from an acquaintance or a fellow buggy enthusiast, basically someone who can personally verify its condition. Should you be acquiring

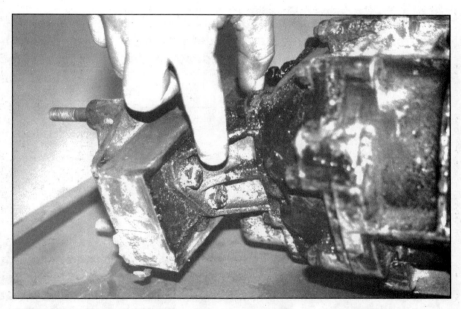

When buying a used transmission, such as this 1973 VW bug tranny, visually inspect the unit for obvious signs of damage or abuse, such as broken mounting points, especially the front mounting bracket and the front rubber mount.

Next, check the rear output spline, clutch cross shaft, and clutch forks for excessive wear or bends.

Also check both the front seal (left) and rear seal (right) for gear oil leakage.

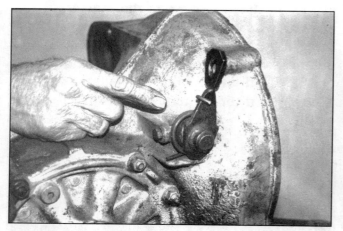

Now check the clutch return spring and make sure it's not cracked or broken. A crack in the return spring can be tough to spot, so inspect it closely, and if you buy a transmission and find a cracked or broken spring, replace it before you install the transmission in your dune buggy.

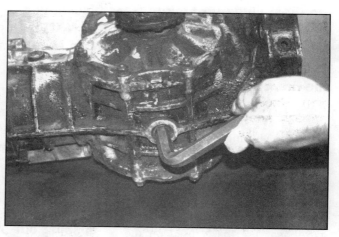

The first step in checking out the used transmission you've bought is to lay it on its side (either one) and with either a 17-mm or 11/16-inch Allen wrench, remove both bottom transmission drain plugs.

a used transmission from a swap meet vendor, or a private individual thru a classified ad, visually inspect the transmission for obvious signs of damage or abuse, such as broken mounting points, particularly the front mounting bracket and front rubber mount.

It is highly recommended that a new rubber front mount be used, because if you leave an old rubber mount on the transmission, install the transmission in your buggy and two months later it goes bad, it turns into a real project to replace the mount. And I mean a real project, including removal of the engine, both

axles, the shift coupler, the starter wires, the transmission, etc. Then you still have to replace the defective mount, and put it all back together again. Is it really worth taking a chance on a used transmission mount?

Then check the rear output spline and clutch cross shaft and forks for excessive wear, bending, etc. Also, check both the front and rear seals for gear oil leakage, and the clutch return spring for damage or cracks. A crack in the return spring can be tough to spot, so inspect it closely, and if you buy a transmission and find a cracked or broken spring

replace it before you install the transmission in your dune buggy.

If you do locate what appears to be a good used transmission, the first thing to do is lay the transmission on either side and with a 17-mm or 11/16-inch Allen wrench remove both bottom transmission drain plugs (some transmissions have only one drain plug), and inspect the magnets that are built into the drain plugs for evidence of broken transmission gear teeth or excessive metal wear. A very slight amount of metal particles is normal.

One more item to inspect for wear is the starter bushing. If you see

Also, inspect the magnets that are built into the drain plugs for broken transmission gear teeth or excessive metal particles. NOTE: A very slight amount of metal particles is normal. Also, some transmissions have only one drain plug.

One more item to inspect for wear is the starter bushing. If you see the starter bushing worn excessively — to the point of being egg shaped — it must be replaced before installing a new starter. Should you find that your starter bushing is bad, replace it now, not after it's mounted in the buggy.

the starter bushing worn excessively, such as to the point of being egg shaped, it must be replaced before installing a new starter.

The starter bushing size determines whether a 6-volt or 12-volt starter was previously used on the transmission. From past experience, I can say a 12-volt system is the only way to go.

Should you find your starter bushing bad replace it now, not after it's mounted in the buggy. To replace the starter bushing, first drive the old bushing out of the transmission housing. This is done by using a 6-inch 3/8-inch drive extension with a socket on it that will go through the housing without getting stuck. After carefully removing the old bushing, we installed the new one by inserting it in the housing and properly seating it with a bushing installer. If you don't have a bushing installer, you can make your own by using a 3/8-inch bolt with a nut screwed onto it. Be sure to insert the bushing from the same direction that the starter is installed. These bushings are very fragile, so take care when installing them.

If by chance you are using a 6-volt transmission, and you want to

We replaced our starter bushing by first driving the old bushing out of the transmission housing. This was accomplished by using a

3-inch 3/8- drive extension with a socket on it that went through the housing without getting stuck.

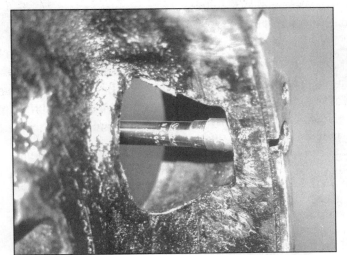

We installed the new bushing by inserting it in the housing and properly seating it with a bushing installer.

use a 12-volt starter, you can purchase a 6 to 12-volt replacement starter bushing. However, if it's at all possible, try to locate a VW Bug transmission of 1968 or newer vintage, which should guarantee you of a 12-volt unit. If you purchase what appears to be, and is claimed to be, a good used transmission, ask the seller if he will replace the unit or refund your money if the unit proves to be defective. Should he agree to this, it's smart to get it in writing.

Finally, if you do not locate a good used transmission, there's always the option of buying a rebuilt one. Rebuilt VW Bug transmissions are plentiful, reasonably priced, and usually come with a warranty. TIP: If your budget permits, this is the best option. When you go the rebuilt route you can be reasonably assured that the transmission will be in good working order. When buying a rebuilt unit be sure to specify that a 12-volt starter will be used.

Now let's get started with our project transmission. Being a used unit, it started out in fine working order but needed a good cleaning and painting. We started by wire brushing the entire unit, front to rear. Then with compressed air and with our safety goggles on, we blew out all the cracks and crevices. Now with all the dirt and scale removed, we gave it a fresh coat of aluminum color spray paint. It looked like a new one.

Next, we installed a new front rubber mount, which, when the transmission is installed, will bolt up to the previously installed rear torsion. Then came our solid rear mount, which will also support a part of our rear buggy frame. We installed the mount by inserting the rear torsion mount bolts through the mount and securing it to the rear torsion horns by tightening the bolts. Then we followed this checklist before installing the transmission:

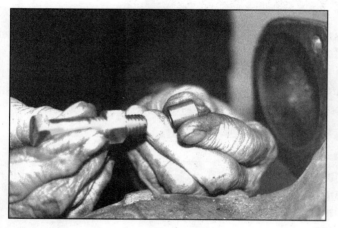

If you don't have a bushing installer, make your own by using a 3/8-inch bolt with a nut screwed on it.

Be sure to insert the bushing from the same direction that the starter is installed, or it won't seat properly. The starter can go in only one way, while the bushing can be installed from either direction, but only one is correct. This bushing is very fragile, so take care when installing it.

If you are using a used 6-volt transmission and you want to use a 12-volt starter, you can purchase a 6 to 12-volt replacement starter bushing.
Shown here are a 12-volt bushing for a 12-volt transmission (right), and a 12-volt conversion bushing for use in a 6-volt transmission (left). But try to locate a VW Bug transmission that is 1968 or later, which assures you of a 12-volt unit.

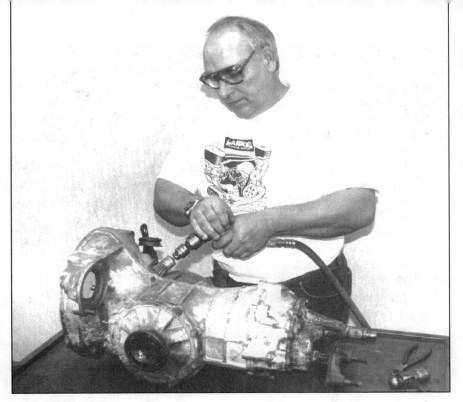

- Are both front and rear mounts installed and secure?
- Is the backup light switch installed?
- Are the clutch shaft and fork installed and working properly?
- Did we change the transmission gear oil, and if so did we use 80/90w gear oil?
- Is the transmission fluid level at the full mark?

Now everything was ready for the installation of our transmission. We started by sliding the transmission under the rear of the buggy, with the large opening of the unit (the end the engine mates to) facing the rear of the buggy. Then by lifting the front of the transmission upward enough to clear the solid rear mount, a friend carefully installed the front

Our used transmission started out in good working order, but needing a good cleaning and painting. Fitted with safety glasses, Bill Fast wire brushed the entire unit, front to rear, and then with compressed air blew out all the cracks and crevices.

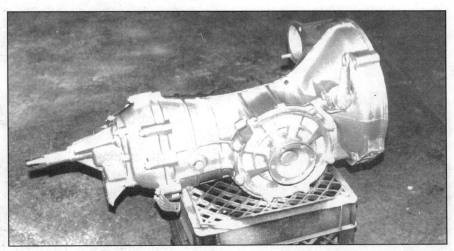

Now with all the dirt and scale removed, Fast gave it a fresh new coat of aluminum color spray paint. Check out how our nasty looking used transmission was transformed into a like new beauty.

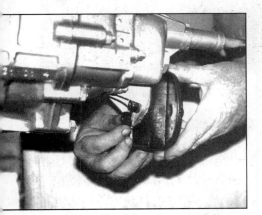

Next, we installed a new front rubber mount, which, when the transmission is installed, will bolt up to the previously installed rear torsion.

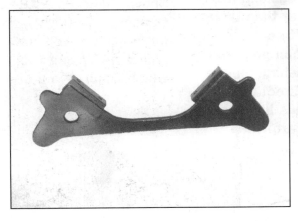

Then came this solid rear mount, which will also support a part of our rear buggy frame.

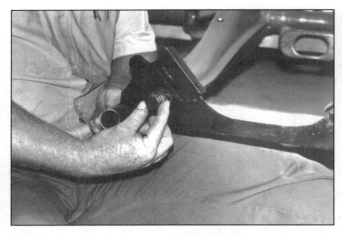

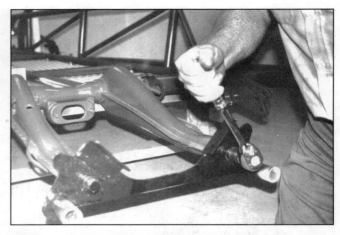

We installed this mount by inserting the rear torsion mount bolts (above, left) through the mount and securing it to the rear torsion horns and tightening it down (above, right). Before installing the transmission, make sure that both front and rear mounts are secure, the backup light switch (below, right) has been installed, the clutch shaft and clutch fork have been installed and are working properly, the transmission gear oil is fresh and full, and if the fluid has been changed, a quality 80/90w gear oil has been used.

rubber mount onto the two studs sticking out of the front torsion, and then set the rear of the transmission on the solid mount.

With the transmission cradled on its mounts, we then installed washers and nuts on the front mount and secured them. The last bolts installed were the four that go through the rear of the transmission and then through the solid mount. After securing these bolts, our transmission was installed and ready to be partnered with the engine, axles, shift coupler and the shift tube. ■

To install the transmission, we started by sliding it under the rear of the buggy with the transmission's large opening (where the engine will mount) facing the rear of the buggy.

After lifting the front of the transmission upward far enough to clear the solid rear mount, Randy Hamilton carefully installed the front rubber mount (arrow) onto the two studs sticking out of the front torsion.

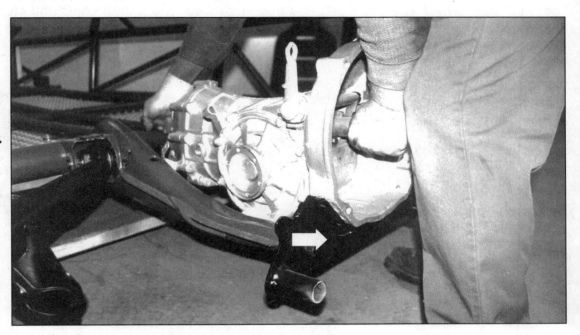

Hamilton then placed the rear of the transmission on the solid mount (arrow).

With the transmission cradled on its mounts, he then installed washers and nuts on the front mount (left) and secured them (right).

The last bolts that Randy installed were the four that went through the rear of the transmission and the solid rear mount (above). After securing these bolts (top, right), our transmission was now installed and ready to be hooked up with the axles (right), shift coupler (below, right), and the engine and shift tube. (The engine and shift tube have not been installed at this point.)

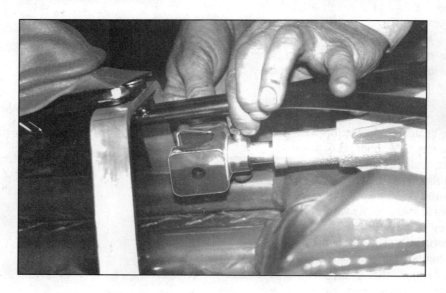

Repacking Rear Axle CV Joints

Rejuvenating Used Components

The best running engine and transmission combination in the world won't help at all if the power doesn't get to the wheels, and that's the job of the rear axles. They need to be up to the task at hand ... period!

New rear axles are great if your budget allows it, and even over-the-counter rebuilt units will work fine. But the least expensive route is to pick up used units that require some attention but are rebuildable. These can be found at VW swap meets, salvage yards and through local trader papers.

Axle boots can be cracked and the overall condition poor, but the CV joints themselves must be usable. The axles must be straight and the CV joints must be reasonably tight. Always use new CV boots as these are critical to satisfactory axle performance. CV boots keep dirt, water and other contaminants out of the CV joints, and keep the grease in the joints where they lubricate the ball bearings and other components.

Follow the accompanying photos and captions for the recommended procedures for testing, disassembling, rebuilding, reassembling and installing the axles. ∎

The rear axles (arrows) that went into the project dune buggy started out as used units that needed some attention.

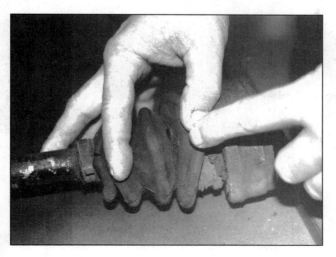

To begin with, the axle boots were cracked. Also, the overall condition was poor. But the CV joints themselves checked out as rebuildable.

To test a used CV joint in a VW Bug rear axle, start by gripping the axle shaft itself with one hand and holding it tightly.

Then with the other hand, grip the outer diameter of the CV joint itself and rock the CV joint in a clockwise and counter-clockwise rotation (arrows). A good CV joint will have very minimal movement in the joint itself.

Then move the CV joint in a rocking forward and backward motion (arrows). There should be no excessive resistance when doing this. NOTE: Be careful not to move the CV joint to extremes in one direction or the other because it could possibly separate and come apart. If one of the joints should come apart, follow the reassembly directions found in any VW Bug shop manual.

We disassembled our axle shafts by first removing all the axle retaining bolts and the outer retaining clips at both ends.

With these clips off, we used a plastic-head hammer to gently tap the back of each CV joint until it separated from the axle.

Now remove the old CV boots. The purpose of a CV boot is to keep water and dirt out of the CV joint and keep grease in the CV joint. We have now disassembled one rear axle shaft. We will proceed to disassemble the remaining axle shaft using the same procedure. NOTE:

Once the CV joints are off, remove the washers that are now visible on the axle shaft.

Because all four CV joints are the same size, it was not necessary to mark the exact locations from which they were removed.

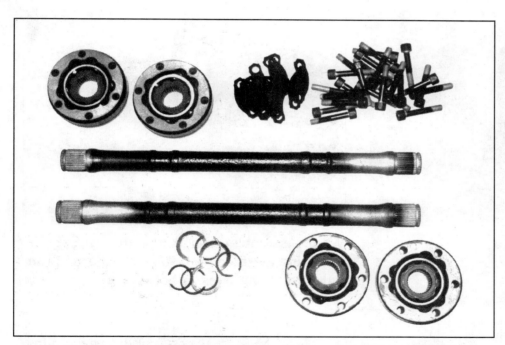

With both axles disassembled, we took all of the old parts and gave them a thorough cleaning. We also sanded and painted the two axle shafts and painted the outside of the CV joint. Take care not to get any paint on the CV bearings.

We purchased new CV joint boots so it was not necessary to clean or try to save any of the old CV boots.

We're now ready to begin reassembling our axles. First, we applied lubrication to the small end of the CV boots.

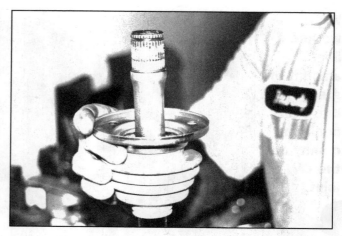

Then with the axle in a bench vise, we installed the CV boot by sliding it down over the axle. When in its proper position, it should look like this.

With both boots installed, our axle looked like this.

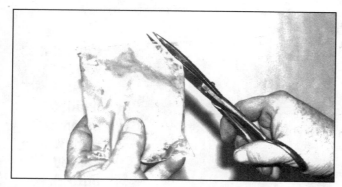

It's now time to open a packet of our special CV joint grease. This special lube is available at most auto parts stores. NOTE: Before you repack any CV joint make absolutely sure it is clean, dry and void of any cleaning solvent. Cleaning solvent will react with the grease and destroy its lubricating ability.

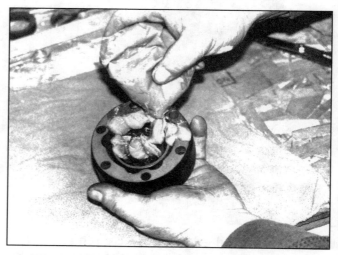

We started repacking the CV joint by squeezing the grease into the CV joint bearings.

We worked a liberal amount of grease into every nook and cranny of the CV joint.

After the CV joint was packed with grease, we put some additional CV grease into the CV boot.

Then we installed the flat washer onto the axle shaft.

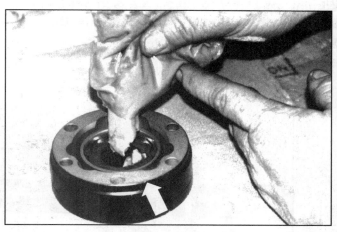

Before installing the CV joint, be aware that there is a proper way for the CV joint to go on the shaft. That is, the beveled edge goes to the outside or away from the CV boot (arrow).

With the beveled edge of the CV joint pointing outward, we installed the CV joint on the splined axle shaft.

Then we tapped it with a plastic-headed hammer until it was seated onto the shaft.

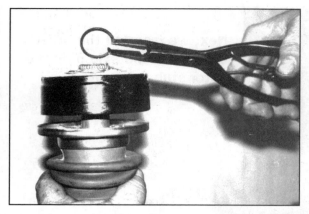

Next, we reinstalled the outer CV joint clip into the groove on the axle shaft. We then reinstalled the cleaned axle bolts and clips, thereby finishing one end of one axle.

We then repeated the same procedure on the other end of the axle and then had one complete axle finished. After repeating the same procedure on the other axle, both axles were now ready to install onto the transmission and outer torsion arm stub axles.

We started by connecting either end of one axle to the transmission.

Then we started the axle retaining bolts by hand and secured them to the transmission.

Next we inserted the other CV joint of the axle onto the outer stub axle (arrow).

We also started those bolts by hand before securing them to the outer stub axle using a ratchet and socket.

After the final bolt tightening, we now had a very clean and workable axle shaft. Repeat this procedure for the other side of the dune buggy. NOTE: The proper procedure is to torque axle bolts to factory specs.

Installing the Clutch Tube and Cable, and the Accelerator Tube and Cable

Hooking It All Up

The installation of the clutch tube and cable and the accelerator tube and cable is a rather basic procedure requiring only common hand tools, plus a vise to be used in bending the clutch tube. There are, however, a number of parts that will be needed.

The parts required to install the clutch cable are:

- 1 clutch cable - Standard VW Bug
- 1 clutch cable tube
- 1 Bowden tube
- 1 cable shortening kit
- 2 eyelet bolts
- 1 electrical cable clamp (available at electrical supply stores)
- 1 small cable clamp

After cutting our tube to proper length, we put a slight bend about two inches inward on the end that will be at the clutch pedal, we next drilled a 5/16-inch hole in the frame tube on the floor pan of the buggy. This hole was drilled approximately five inches from the clutch pedal. We then located and drilled another 5/16-inch hole in the frame tube at the shifter box for the installation of the tube holding clamp and one more eyelet bolt. We installed both eyelet bolts onto the clutch tube making sure the rear eyelet had the tube clamp with it. We then inserted both eyelet bolts through the frame tube in the previously drilled holes. **NOTE: Do not secure the eyelet bolts that protrude through the bottom of the frame tube at this time.**

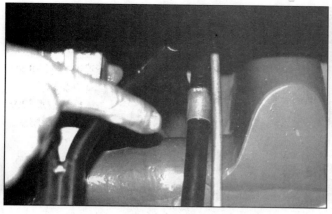

We then slid the clutch cable tube through the eyelet bolts back to the transmission and installed our Bowden tube. The female end of the Bowden tube connects to our clutch cable tube.

The male end of the Bowden tube goes into the transmission Bowden tube guide (arrow).

With the Bowden tube in place and a slight bow in the Bowden tube (arrow), we then secured the clutch cable tube to the frame by securely tightening the two eyelet bolts under the buggy's frame tube.

The necessary parts for the accelerator cable installation are:

- 1 accelerator cable tube
- 1 accelerator cable - Standard VW Bug
- 1 accelerator cable shortening kit
- 5 nylon cable ties
- 1 rubber coated metal cable clamp

In scouting for a proper clutch cable tube, I found that my primary parts supplier, Larry's Off Road Center, had an adequate supply of both clutch cable tubes and accelerator cable tubes. Both of the tubes come in a length that is quite sufficient to fit most dune buggies. Alternative suppliers of such tubes are metal fabrication shops, salvage yards that deal in scrap metal, farm supply stores, and automotive parts stores. The measurement that was needed for our clutch cable tube was 53 inches, but this measurement will vary from frame to frame, and is calculated by allowing approximately three inches of space from the end of the tube to the clutch cable hook on the clutch pedal, and also allowing enough length at the rear of the tube to put a slight bow in the Bowden tube, which connects to the side of the transmission.

These tubes have an outside diameter of 3/8-inch and are made of very sturdy metal, which is

Next, we tightened the tube clamp adjusting bolt.

required because of the heavy pressure put on the cable and tube when operating the clutch. After cutting our tube to the proper length, we put a slight bend about two inches inward on the end that will be at the clutch pedal. NOTE: The reason for putting a slight bend in both the clutch cable tube and the accelerator cable tube is to avoid kinking or binding the cables that will be installed inside them.

We then drilled a 5/16-inch hole in the frame tube on the floor pan of the buggy. This hole was drilled approximately five inches from the clutch pedal. We then located and drilled another 5/16-inch hole in the frame tube at the shifter box for the installation of the tube holding clamp and one more eyelet bolt. We installed both eyelet bolts onto the clutch tube making sure the rear eyelet had the tube clamp with it.

We then inserted both eyelet bolts through the frame tube in the previously drilled holes. NOTE: Do not secure the eyelet bolts that protrude through the bottom of the frame tube at this time.

We then slid the clutch cable tube through the eyelet bolts back to the transmission and installed our Bowden tube. The female end of the Bowden tube connects to our clutch cable tube and the male end of the Bowden tube goes into the transmission Bowden tube guide. With this in place and a slight bow in the Bowden tube, we then secured the clutch cable tube to the frame by securely tightening the two eyelet bolts under the buggy's frame tube and then tightening the tube clamp adjusting bolt.

Next, we inserted the new clutch cable through the front section of the clutch cable tube and pushed it out the rear end of the tube. We proceeded to hook up the eyelet end of the clutch cable to the clutch pedal. We

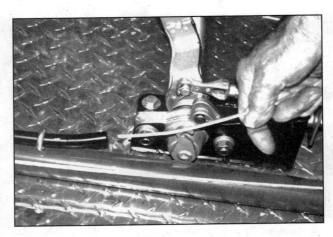

We then inserted the new clutch cable through the front section of the clutch cable tube and pushed it out the rear end of the tube.

We proceeded to hook up the eyelet end of the clutch cable to the clutch pedal (arrow).

If the cable is hooked up properly, it will look like this.

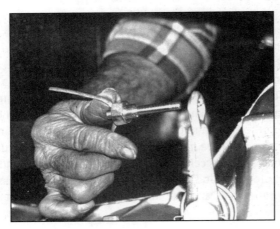

We then took the clutch cable end at the transmission and installed the cable shortening kit. (NOTE: Allow approximately two inches of excess cable through the shortening kit.) After installing the cable through the cable shortening kit, we then tightened the large nut to secure the cable to the shortening kit.

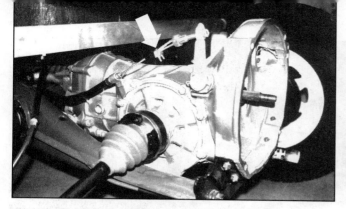

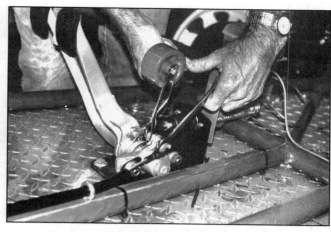

Also, for added protection against cable slippage we installed a small cable clamp (arrow). We then inserted the clutch cable adjusting rod through the clutch release arm and installed one adjusting rod nut and flat washer, but did not adjust the clutch at this time. That will be done after the engine and new clutch have been installed on the transmission.

With the clutch cable and tube installed we then installed our roller accelerator pedal on the clutch and brake assembly using the proper bolt and nut to secure it in place.

We used a 70-inch length of 1/4-inch metal brake line to construct the accelerator tube. We then put a slight curve at the accelerator pedal end, and then positioned it to the frame alongside the clutch cable tube and ran it all the way to the transmission where it hooked into the engine accelerator cable tube (right). We then used nylon tie straps at different locations to secure the accelerator tube to the frame, plus one metal cable clamp (as seen here), which we secured to one of the emergency brake supports.

then took the clutch cable end at the transmission and installed the cable shortening kit. NOTE: Allow approximately two inches of excess cable through the shortening kit. After installing the cable through the cable shortening kit, we tightened the large nut to secure the cable to the shortening kit. In addition, for added protection against cable slippage, we installed a small cable clamp.

We inserted the clutch cable

adjusting rod through the clutch release arm and installed one adjusting rod nut and flat washer but did not adjust the clutch at this time. That will be done after the engine and new clutch have been installed on the transmission. With the clutch cable and tube mounted, we installed our roller accelerator pedal on the clutch and brake assembly using the proper bolt and nut to secure it in place.

The accelerator tube was much easier to install than the clutch cable tube because there were no holes to drill, no eyelets to install, and we used simple cable ties to secure it to the frame. We used a 70-inch length of 1/4-inch metal brake line, put a slight curve at the accelerator pedal end, and then positioned it on the frame alongside the clutch cable tube and ran it all the way to the transmission, where it hooked into the

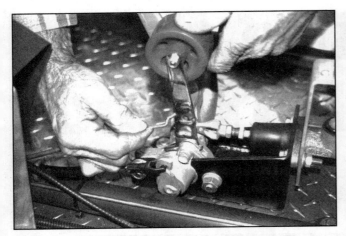

To finish up our accelerator cable and tube we then ran the accelerator cable through the accelerator tube and took the S-hook end of the cable and installed it into the hole in the accelerator pedal. We proceeded to push the remaining cable through the tube until it came out the other end at the carburetor.

Here's the completed installation of the S-hook end.

engine accelerator cable tube. We then used nylon tie straps at different locations to secure the accelerator tube to the frame, plus one metal cable clamp was used to affix it to one of the emergency brake supports.

To finish up our accelerator cable and tube we then ran the accelerator cable through the accelerator tube and took the S-hook end of the cable and installed it into the hole in the accelerator pedal. We proceeded to push the remaining cable through the tube until it came out the other end at the carburetor.

Finally, we used an accelerator cable shortening kit to facilitate the proper length cable and installed it at the carburetor throttle. The finished installation was neat and fully functional. ■

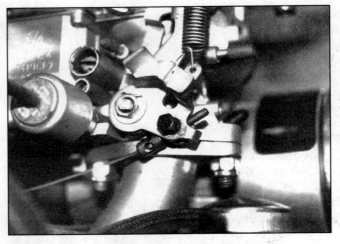

Finally, we used an accelerator cable shortening kit to hold the cable, which had been cut to proper length, and installed it at the carburetor throttle. With the accelerator tube and cable installed properly, the finished result looks like this.

Installing the Shifter Box and Shift Tube

A Matter of Ergonomics

There are many different variations of shifter boxes, including the weld-on and bolt-on types. The weld-on type can be welded into place either by the frame manufacturer or you, assuming you have the proper welding equipment at your disposal and the knowledge and experience to weld safely. The problem with having it welded on by the manufacturer is that once it is welded into place, it becomes difficult to move should you discover that the shifter box is not located within easy reach of the driver's seating position. It's simply a matter of automotive ergonomics (the relationship of man to his driving environment).

I would heartily suggest that the bolt-on type be used, especially if the buggy builder is a rookie, or if he doesn't have access to welding equipment. I have always used the bolt-on type with great success.

Manufacturing the brackets that mount to the shifter box and then to the floor pan was rather simple and easy. I took aluminum angle, or L-shaped stock which was 1-1/4 inch by 1-1/4 inch and then measured the shifter box ends and cut two pieces of aluminum angle to that

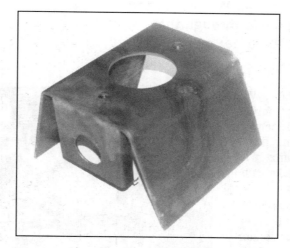

There are several types of shifter boxes, such as this weld-on type, which can be welded in place either by the frame manufacturer or, if you have access to the proper welding equipment, you can tackle it yourself.

It is highly recommended that the novice use the bolt-on type of shifter box.

measurement. I then drilled 5/16-inch holes in the two brackets and the box and then drilled corresponding holes in the floor pan. We then mounted the unit to the floor pan.

Another part of the shifter box

that is very important is the nylon bushing for the shift tube. This is very easy to install as long as the shift tube has not yet been installed. The shift tube slides through it. I had a local machine shop manufacture an adjustable shift rod tube to my speci-

After making the mounting brackets for the shifter box, we mounted the brackets to the box and then installed the box on the floor pan.

The nylon bushing for the shift tube is a critical piece, but is very easy to install before the shift tube is inserted, as seen here. The shift tube slides through it.

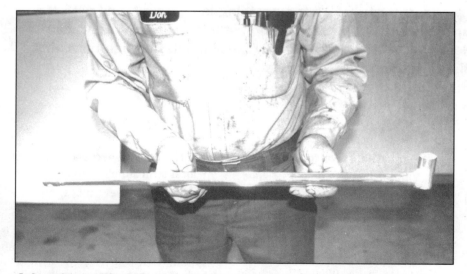

A local machine shop manufactured the shift tube to my specifications.

fications. These are not available over the parts counter and will have to be custom manufactured.

The manufacture of a shift rod tube can be time consuming and even frustrating. Before measuring exact lengths, manufacturing any parts, or installing the finished product, the shifter box and the transmission must be permanently installed. The traditional way of manufacturing a shift tube is, with the shifter box and tranny installed, measure from the center of the round hole in the shifter box, to the center of the shift coupler that has been installed on the transmission shift rod. (CAUTION: The transmission must be in neutral to make this measurement.)

After these measurements have been calculated and recorded, take a stock shift tube that has been salvaged from a VW Bug parts car (standard shift only), cut the tube in half, lay both pieces side by side and measure from the center of the ball socket end to the center of the drilled hole in the other end. This measurement must equal the first measurement that was arrived at and recorded.

With the two pieces held securely to avoid any change in length, mark both pieces at a point close to the smaller end. The next step is to cut both pieces where marked to arrive at the total length first calculated. When this has been done, hold both pieces together and hold them slightly above the shift box and the transmission shift couple and visually check for proper measurement. If everything looks good, the two separate pieces must now be welded to form one complete tube.

It is critical to check for proper location of the two pieces before welding. With the (ball socket) end pointing straight up, the drilled hole in the other piece must be perfectly parallel with the ball socket. With the two pieces properly aligned, welding can now be done. CAUTION: A professional-quality weld is of critical importance, because a strong and permanent weld is necessary, not only for adequate strength

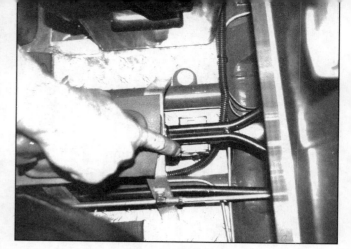

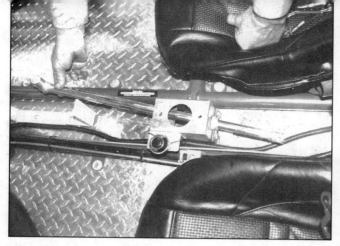

The adjustable shift rod tube was inserted through the front of the shifter box and the nylon bushing by pushing it from the front to the rear, with the end that has the drilled hole pointing toward the transmission.

After the tube was installed, I hooked it up to the transmission shift fork coupler.

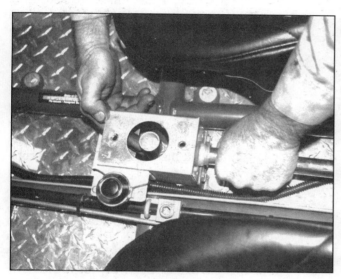

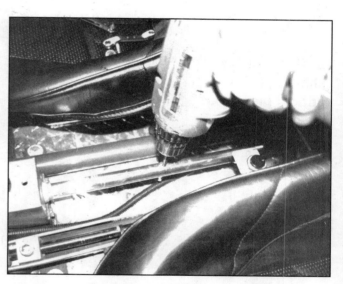

With the tube in place it is very important to position the front shift tube cup in the center of the shifter box, and level the rear shift coupler so that it is parallel to the floor pan. NOTE: The transmission must be in the neutral position when performing this installation.

After everything is centered, and with the transmission still in neutral, we carefully drilled a 5/16-inch hole through both shift rod tubes.

but also to ensure that it is flat and smooth enough to slip through the shift bushing that is installed in the shifter box. If any burrs or protrusions extend from the welded area, they must be sanded or filed smooth before inserting the tube into the bushing. If your calculations are wrong, the only thing to do is cut the tube and either shorten it or length-

en it and have it rewelded.

With all this in mind, I decided to try to come up with a simpler design that would be easier to install and adjust. I started by locating two pieces of aluminum tubing; the first one had to have the same diameter as the outside diameter of the original VW Bug shift tube. The second tube had to slide snugly inside the first

tube. I found the necessary tubes at my local farm supply store.

I took both new tubes, and the original shift tube, to a local machine shop and had them fabricate two ends that were similar to the original tube ends. With these new ends finished, they then professionally welded them onto the new tubes that I had provided. But before welding, I

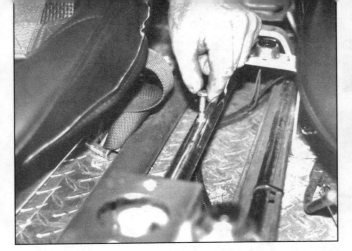

We then secured the shift rod tubes with a bolt, lock washer and nut.

Next, we put a small amount of thick grease, such as wheel bearing grease, in the cup of the shift rod tube.

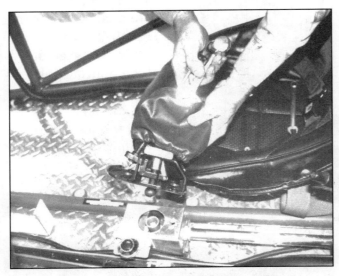

We then proceeded with the installation of the shifter, and adjusted the shifter according to the instructions supplied with it.

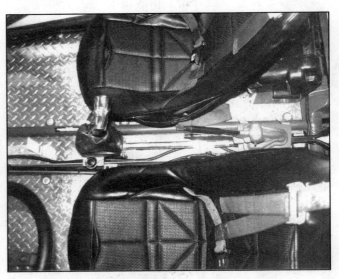

The completed installation looks greats, works fine and should prove very durable.

made certain that they put the ball socket end on the larger of the tubes. With this accomplished and back at the shop, I proceeded to measure from the center of the shifter box to within approximately 12 inches of the shift coupler on the transmission. I then cut the tube with the ball socket to this length. (This length will vary depending on the location of the shifter box.)

Next I cut the smaller tube to a length of 30 inches, which was quite adequate for the 12-inch space between the end of the larger tube and the shift coupler. It also assured a sufficient length of the smaller tube,

so it would slide inside the larger tube. With both tubes put together, I now have a workable and adjustable shift rod tube, and can proceed with the installation of this tube.

The adjustable shift rod tube is inserted through the front of the shifter box and the nylon bushing by pushing it from the front to the rear, with the end that has the drilled hole pointing toward the transmission.

After the tube was installed, I hooked it up to the transmission shift fork coupler. With the tube in place it is very important to position the front shift tube cup in the center of the shifter box, and level the rear shift

coupler so that it is parallel to the floor pan. NOTE: The transmission must be in the neutral position when performing this installation.

After everything is centered, and with the transmission still in neutral, we carefully drilled a 5/16-inch hole through both shift rod tubes and secured them with a bolt, lock washer and nut. Next, we put a small amount of thick grease, such as wheel bearing grease, in the cup of the shift rod tube. We then proceeded with the installation of our shifter and adjusted the shifter in accordance with the instructions that came with it. ∎

Installing the Shock Absorbers

Ironing Out the Bumps

Shock absorbers play a critical role in the performance of the suspension system, ironing out those bumps and potholes, while helping the driver maintain control of his buggy and giving both driver and passenger a relatively comfortable ride. Quality shocks are worth the extra expense in the long run as they not only perform better but last longer.

To install the front shocks, which were stock VW Bug units, we started by mounting the bottom of the shock over the lower shock stud mount, as seen here.

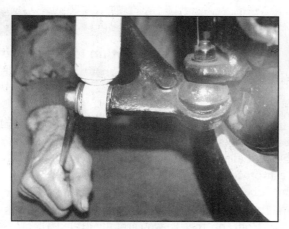

Then we secured the lower shock mount with a flat washer, lock washer and nut. The top of the shock has a 3/8-inch stud that will stick through the top of the shock tower, which is built into the VW Bug front suspension.

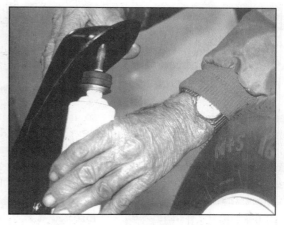

It is important to install a washer on the upper shock stud first, then a new rubber grommet before inserting the shock through the hole in the shock tower.

After we inserted the stud through the hole in the shock tower (right), we then placed the remaining rubber grommet and our pre-made light bar on the top of both shocks and then (far right) the lock washer and nut.

 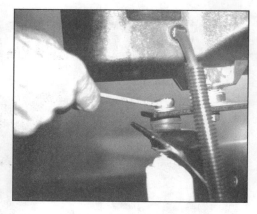

Rear shock installation was more of a challenge since we wanted to install the upper shock mounts without welding. We solved the problem by using Coleman clamps. First, we located a clamp on the rear frame support bar at a specific distance from the lower shock mount,

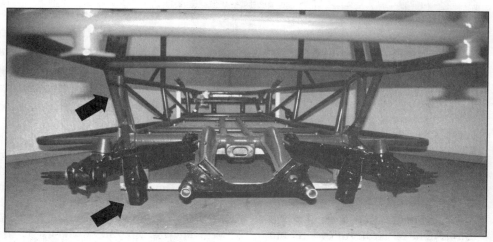

to prevent the shock from going beyond its fully extended position. Shown here is the lower shock mount (bottom arrow) with the upper shock mounting location noted (top arrow).

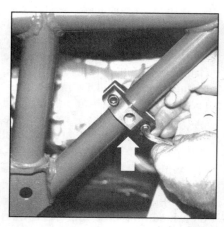 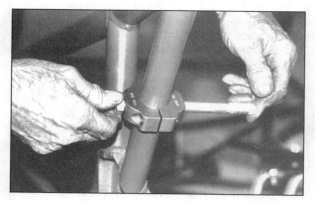

After drilling a 1/2-inch hole through the clamp and frame tube, we inserted our 1/2x6 upper shock bolt through the clamp and frame tube.

After selecting our mounting location, we then installed our Coleman clamp to the frame bar and tightened it in place. The arrow indicates where we will drill for the installation of the upper shock bolt.

When we installed the shock on the upper shock mount, it was determined that we would need spacers to adjust the shock outward from the clamp approximately 1-1/4 inches, so the shock would be in a vertical position.

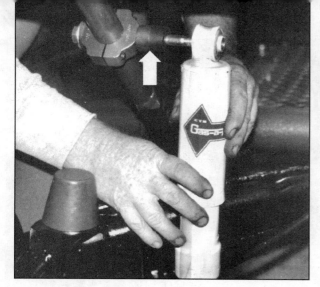

So we installed the necessary spacers (arrow), which figured to a pair of them in our installation.

With our shock secured to the upper shock mount, we proceeded to bolt the bottom of the shock to the shock housing. Actually, the shock slides down into the housing and is locked in place with a bolt passing through the housing and the shock mount. TIP: Always use a flat washer and a lock washer to avoid having the nut vibrate loose.

The front shocks that we selected for our project buggy were readily available stock shocks designed to fit a 1973 VW Bug. The installation of these shocks is reasonably simple and can be done either before or after the front suspension has been bolted in place.

We started by installing the bottom of the shock over the lower shock mounting stud and securing it with a flat washer, lock washer and nut. The top of the shock has a 3/8-inch stud that will stick through the top of the shock tower, which is built onto the front suspension. NOTE: It is important to install a washer on the upper shock stud first, then a new rubber grommet before inserting it through the hole in the shock tower.

After we inserted the upper shock stud through the hole in the shock tower, we placed the remaining rubber grommet and our pre-made light bar on the top of both shocks and then secured them with the lock washer and nut.

By keeping in mind that there is additional stress on the rear suspension due to the weight of the engine and transmission, we purchased heavy duty gas-charged shocks. The rear shock installation was a bit more difficult as there was no mounting

point for the upper end of our shocks. Further complicating things were these factors: Our frame had already been painted, we didn't have a wire welder, and we preferred not to weld anyway. So, the challenge was to install an upper shock mount without welding. To drill a hole through the frame tube and insert a long shock bolt through the tube would not have been strong enough to meet the demands put on the shocks by the extra weight of the engine and transmission.

Our ready made Coleman clamps were the obvious choice for accomplishing our task. The first thing we did was to locate the clamp on the rear frame support bar at a specific distance from the lower shock mount, to ensure that the shock could not go beyond its fully extended position. With the frame elevated off the floor, the rear torsion arms were fully extended in their down position. By allowing approximately one inch of space before full extension of the shocks themselves, we can avoid damage to the shocks if or when we want to do some moderate off roading.

We determined the mounting location then installed our Coleman clamp to the frame bar and tightened it. After drilling a 1/2-inch hole

through the clamp and frame tube, we inserted our 1/2x6 upper shock bolt through the clamp and frame tube. NOTE: With this upper shock bolt we allowed an additional 1/2-inch length for the purpose of having a point to secure the metal brace that will be used to support the rear of our soon-to-be-installed storage box.

When we installed the shock on the upper shock mount, it was decided that we would need spacers to adjust the shock outward from the clamp approximately 1-1/4 inches, so the shock would be in a vertical position. Our application required two spacers on each rear shock. Spacers can be acquired at most local auto parts stores.

With our shocks mounted on the upper shock mounts, we proceeded to bolt the bottom of the shocks into their mounting position. TIP: Always use a flat washer and a lock washer to avoid having the nut vibrate loose.

NOTE: If you plan to install a storage box in a location similar to the one used for the storage box on the project dune buggy, do not secure the upper shock nuts at this time as the storage box brace will be fastened to both shocks when mounting the storage box. ∎

Installing the Front and Rear Lights

An Illuminating Subject

Not only are front and rear lights mandatory for any street-driven dune buggy, they're imperative if night-time operation is desired, either on or off road. Buggies used strictly off-road, such as in racing and other competitions, may not require lights at all. The dune buggy builder should first consult state and local authorities to make sure that the type of lighting being considered complies with current laws in effect where he will be operating his buggy.

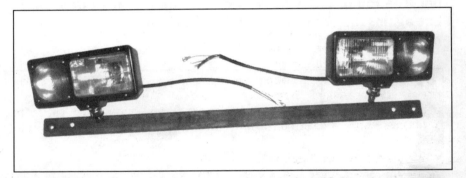

We selected low-profile snowplow headlights for our buggy project. These units, which are readily available at most automotive parts stores, include high beam, low beam, turn signals, parking lights, and all necessary wiring in one compact system.

The most common locations for mounting front lights and turn signals are the front suspension and the front shock towers; here the lights are mounted on the front shock towers.

Another popular mounting position is the windshield frame bar, either on the bottom bar, as seen here, or on the top bar. The top of the window seems to be the most popular, but again, the light mounting location depends upon the buggy builder.

I located the project buggy's headlights on a steel bar mounted atop the front shock towers. To make the mounting bar, I first measured the distance from the outside of one shock tower to the outside of the opposite shock tower.

Let's discuss the light units I chose for the project dune buggy and the reasons I selected them. The headlight units used were low-profile snowplow lights available at many automotive parts stores. These units combine high beam, low beam, turn signals, parking lights, all in one compact unit, complete with all necessary wiring.

These units can be mounted in a variety of locations on any dune buggy frame. The location of your front lights will determine if it will be necessary to weld or bolt mounting tabs on your frame. The most commonly used locations for mounting front lights and turn signals are the front suspension and/or the front shock towers. The window frame bar is another popular mounting position, both on the bottom bar and the top bar. The top of the window seems to be the most popular, but again, the light mounting location depends on the buggy builder. So, use your imagination and go with what looks good and works for you. NOTE: But do keep in mind that the mounting location and bracket must be sturdy and the lights must not interfere with any front suspension movement, including shocks, steering linkage, and tire rotation.

Also, when mounting the front lights, take into consideration that at some point in time you might want to install a front body and hood assembly. The wrong light-mounting location with any front lights can create a real problem in this area. If you mount your lights on the front frame bars or on the top of the front I beam, which is part of the suspension, it rules out the installation of most front hoods and side panels.

So with all this in mind, I located the project buggy's headlights on a steel bar which mounted on top of the front shock towers. To make the mounting bar I first measured the distance from the outside of one shock tower to the outside of the opposite shock tower. After calculating this distance at 40 inches, I transferred these measurements to a section of steel bar measuring 2-inches wide by 1/4-inch thick.

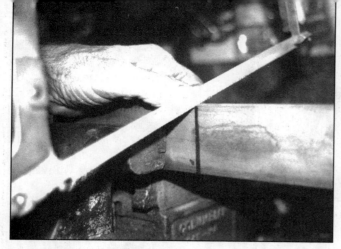

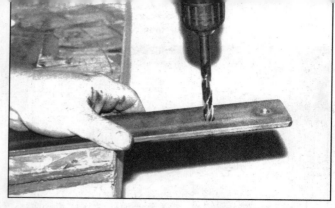

After calculating this distance at 40 inches, I transferred these measurements to a section of steel bar two inches wide by 1/4-inch thick. I then cut the bar with a hack saw and rounded the corners at both ends for safety reasons.

With the bar cut to the correct length, I positioned it on top of the front shock studs and marked these locations. I then drilled a 25/64-inch hole at each end of the bar. This hole must be the same size as the shock stud, so measure the shock stud diameter on your particular front shocks. I also drilled a 3/8-inch hole two inches from the outside hole for mounting the headlight unit, as seen here.

Now we can proceed to sand, clean, primer and paint the light bar the color of our choice, which in this case was black.

After cutting the bar with a hack saw, I rounded the corners at both ends for safety reasons. With the bar cut to the correct length, I positioned the bar on top of the front shock studs and marked these locations. I then drilled a 25/64-inch hole at each end of the bar. NOTE: This hole must be the same size as the shock stud, so measure the shock stud diameter on your particular front shocks.

Next, we sanded, cleaned, primed and painted the light bar; any

After the paint dried, we installed the light bar on the shock studs, using the existing nuts to secure the bar in position. With the light bar in place we can now install our low profile front light assemblies.

Previously, I had a friend hold the light assemblies at different locations on the light bar until I had decided on a permanent spot for the lights. We marked these locations and drilled appropriate size holes to accommodate the mounting stud size of the light assemblies that we chose. In our case the size of the hole was 3/8-inch.

We were now ready to mount the lights, aim them, and secure them to the light bar.

color can be used. After the paint dried, we installed the light bar on the shock studs, using the existing nuts to secure the bar. With the light bar in place we can now locate the position for our low profile front light assemblies. I had a friend hold the light assemblies on the light bar at different locations until a decision was reached on a permanent spot for the lights. We marked these locations and drilled appropriate-sized holes to accommodate the size of the mounting stud for the light assemblies that we used. In our case the hole was 3/8-inch.

Having accomplished this, we can now mount the lights, aim them, and secure them to the light bar. NOTE: It has been my experience that front turn signal lights are more visible if located to the outside of the dune buggy (again check state and local laws for any regulations stipulating light placement).

The back lights I used were truck and trailer rear light assemblies with brake, turn, parking and back-up lights in one unit. By turning the unit horizontally, I used the back-up light bulb for the turn signal. You might wonder why didn't I use the

It has been my experience that front turn signal lights are more visible if located to the outside of the dune buggy (arrow). NOTE: Check state and local laws concerning the location of lights, especially turn signals.

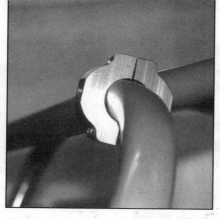

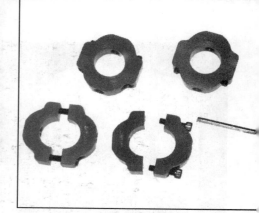

For rear lights I chose truck and trailer rear light assemblies with brake, turn, park and back-up lights in one unit. These are available at most auto parts stores, trailer dealers, discount stores, etc. By turning the unit horizontally I used the back-up light bulb for the turn signal. These units typically come with clear back-up light lenses, but I removed the lens and installed amber-colored tape over the flip side of the back-up lens to comply with Ohio codes.

One alternative for mounting the rear lights required clamping devices that would go around the 1-1/2 inch round frame bar, such as Coleman clamps.

The unique two-piece Coleman clamp fits tightly around the bar. Its two halves tightened together using two Allen head screws and an Allen wrench.

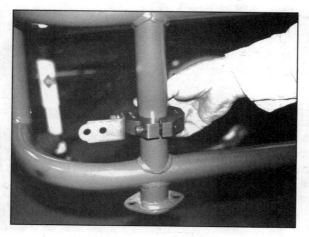

After this clamp has been installed in any number of locations, a simple L-shaped bracket with mounting holes can be bolted to this clamp. This is definitely the easy way out.

one bulb that has two elements in it for the brake and turn signal. The reason is these units were designed for truck and trailer applications where the factory wiring harness has a built-in isolator that separates the brake light from the turn signal in the same bulb. Dune buggies normally do not use a wiring harness of this type.

Later on, we will be installing our own built-from-scratch wiring harness, which incorporates one wire for the left turn signal and a separate wire for the right turn signal, each going to one separate bulb. The same applies for the right and left brake lights, and also a separate wire for the right and left parking lights. The installation of our rear brake, turn and parking light unit was a bit more of a challenge than the front lights. I decided to come up with a different way to mount the rear lights.

After checking local electrical supply houses, automotive retail stores and hardware stores for clamping devices that would go around the 1-1/2 inch round frame bar, I considered using the trusty old Coleman clamp. This unique two-piece clamp fits tightly around the bar by compressing its two halves together around the bar with two Allen head screws. After this clamp has been installed in any number of locations, a simple L-shaped bracket with mounting holes can be bolted to the clamp. This is definitely the easiest and simplest method, but the adventurer in me always likes trying something different.

So I made templates out of poster board to fit the inside curve of the left and right rounded corners of the rear frame bar. I also needed to make templates for both right and left rear

side panels and one for the rear panel. I then took the templates to a local metal fabrication shop where they not only stocked the aluminum diamond plate metal that duplicated the buggy floor pan, they were also able to cut the pieces I needed according to my templates and bend the right and left rear curved panels.

With the rear curved panels completed, a friend held the panels in place, marked and drilled 4-1/16 inch holes thru the panels and frame bar, and secured the panels to the frame using self-tapping Phillips-head screws. With the rear panels in place, my friend held a rear light unit in the center of the installed curved panel and marked the location for drilling the 2-1/4 inch holes necessary for mounting the light unit. He then drilled the 1/4-inch holes in the rear panel. It was also necessary to drill a

However, I always like to do things differently, so I made templates out of poster board to fit the inside curves of the left and right rounded corners of the rear frame bar. At the same time, I made templates for both right and left rear side panels, as well as one for the rear panel.

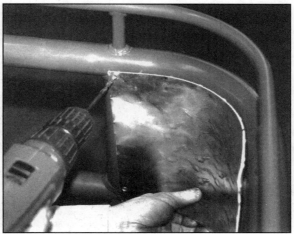

I then took the templates to a local metal fabrication shop where they not only had in stock the aluminum diamond plate metal that matched the buggy floor pan, they were also able to cut the pieces I needed according to my templates and bend the right and left rear curved panels.

3/8-inch hole through which the wiring pigtail would go.

With our holes drilled, my friend, Don McIntosh, inserted the light unit studs through the holes and secured them with the attaching nuts and lock washers supplied with the unit. Don then proceeded to perform the same operation on the other side to mount the second rear light unit. With both curved panels in place and secured we then installed the rear flat panel.

Remember, I had the two flat side panels made at the same time as the other three panels but opted to wait until the buggy was finished to install them. This gave me time to decide if I liked the buggy better with or without the side panels. When it came time to install those two panels they presented no installation problems other than it was necessary to notch both right and left panels with a hack saw and bench grinder at the bottom to make clearance for two Coleman clamps used to hold the bracket for the fuel tank.

After all five panels, including the right and left side flat panels, the flat rear panel, and both the right and left rear corner panels, were mounted, the finished assembly looked great. ■

Now that the rear curved panels were completed, a friend, Don McIntosh, held the panels in place, marked and drilled 4-1/16 inch holes thru the panels and frame bar and secured the panels to the frame using self-tapping Phillips head

This is what the rear panels looked like completely installed.

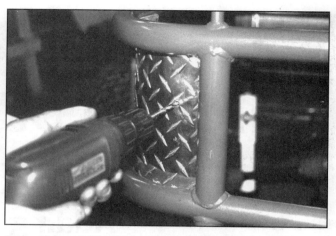

With the rear panels in place, Don held a rear light unit in the center of the installed curved panel and marked the location for drilling the 2-1/4 inch holes necessary for mounting the light unit.

Don then drilled the 1/4-inch holes in the rear panel. NOTE: It was also necessary to drill a 3/8-in hole for the wiring pigtail.

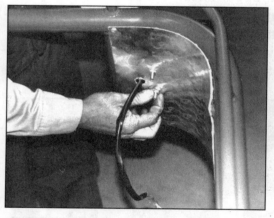

With our holes drilled Don inserted the light unit studs through the holes and secured them with the attaching nuts and lock washers supplied with the unit.

Don then proceeded to perform the same operation on the other side in order to mount the other rear light unit. With both curved panels in place and secured we next installed the rear flat panel. On the three remaining panels, we opted to wait until the buggy was finished to install them.

After all five panels — right and left side flat panels, one flat rear panel, and both right and left rear corner panels — were in place, the finished assembly looked superb. The front and rear lighting units added another finishing touch, and a very functional one.

Installing the Storage Box

Adding a Trunk

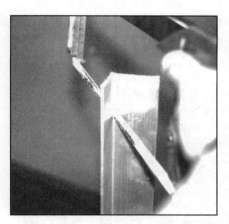

After locating an acceptable storage box of the proper dimensions, the next step was to install the rear support for the box on the buggy. It was simply a matter of measuring the distance between both rear upper shock spacers, adding four inches to the measurement (two inches for each end), and cutting a piece of 2x2 aluminum angle to fit. We put the 2x2 angle in a vise and cut a two-inch slot down each end of the spine or back edge of the angle.

We then placed the angle in a vise so that one of the sides was down and the other side pointing up. We then bent the two ends at a 90-degree angle away from the piece.

It's not uncommon for me to put 200 to 300 miles on a dune buggy in a single weekend, so having a storage box for hauling extra gear, such as food, rain suits, tools, first aid kit, fire extinguisher, etc., comes in handy. On one summer vacation I towed my dune buggy from my home in Ohio to Colorado and had a great time touring the Rocky Mountains, and driving up Pike's Peak Highway. I then towed the buggy to Utah and had a blast traveling the paved roadways and designated off-road trails through the deserts and canyons.

Some national parks have excellent planned four-wheel-drive trails and roads, but if established off-road trails are not available, just driving through a national park on the paved highways in a dune buggy is an expe-rience you will not forget. Obey all park rules and stay on designated roads and highways.

To enter our great national parks with a dune buggy it must be street legal, with proper insurance and valid license plates, essentially the same as with a regular passenger car or light truck.

Having a storage box in a dune buggy is purely an option, actually most dune buggies do not have them, but if you plan on doing any traveling with your buggy, especially extended runs into the desert, by all means consider installing a storage box. They're really handy.

To install a storage box in any dune buggy, the first thing to be done is to measure available space within the frame. A storage box MUST NOT contact or interfere with the fuel tank, battery, seats, or shift linkage.

The usable space for mounting a

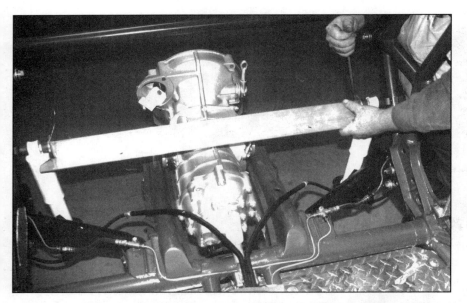

Next we drilled one hole in each end and bolted them to the upper shock mounts. The storage box will sit on the other side of the aluminum angle. It is also necessary to find a mounting point for the front of the storage box.

Fortunately, there is a threaded hole in the VW Bug rear torsion that was used as a body bolt. So, we measured from this location up to level with the upper rear shock bolts. This height came to approximately seven inches.

storage box on our project dune buggy was:

- Rear support area, 36 inches
- Front support area, 41 inches
- Space between the two supports, 15 inches
- Area between seats and engine, maximum height limit, 15 inches

Armed with these measurements, I went scouting for a metal or plastic storage box that would fit within our space limitations. The first stops were the local variety stores and hardware stores, but the storage boxes they carried were either too big or too small. My next stop was a farm supply store, where they carried a nice inventory of storage boxes and had just the one I needed. It measured 32 inches wide, 11-1/2 inches deep, and 12 inches high. Not only a perfect fit with room to spare, but it was also made from very sturdy recycled plastic and had a strong latch that I could secure with a pad lock.

Mounting the storage box is basically a simple procedure that will vary from buggy to buggy. The accompanying photos and captions illustrate and describe the procedure we employed in constructing the support brackets, securing the brackets to the buggy, and installing the storage box. ■

Taking two pieces of 1x1/8 inch wide flat stock, we marked off an 11-inch length.

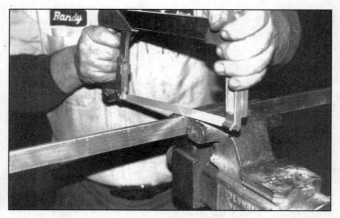

We then cut two pieces of 1x1/8 inch wide flat stock to the pre-measured 11-inch length.

We then measured two inches in on one end of each piece.

We then bolted our two support braces to the rear torsion.

Next, we drilled a 3/8-inch hole in the center of the two-inch end. Then we bent the support brace at a 90-degree angle. We then drilled two 3/8-inch holes in the other end of each piece of our flat stock. We drilled our first hole 1/4-inch in from the end and our second hole 1/2-inch from the first. This end will be bolted to the 2x2 aluminum angle we will be using for the front mounting brace of our storage box. After both front support braces were installed we measured the distance between the braces (from outside to outside) and used this measurement to cut the 2x2 aluminum angle for the front storage box brace. After cutting the brace we drilled 3/8-inch holes in each end of the brace to correspond with the 3/8-inch holes in the support braces.

With both front and rear 2x2 aluminum angle pieces installed, the storage box support system looks like this.

Our precut and predrilled piece of 2x2 aluminum angle was inserted between the two support braces and everything was bolted together.

Randy Hamilton places the storage box inside the dune buggy frame and onto the supports, checking the installation for proper fit and clearance. The box support system required some minor modifications — hand bending the front support braces slightly forward — but other than that there weren't any problems.

Randy then proceeded to drill one 5/16-inch hole in each corner of the storage box and through the 2x2 aluminum angle to facilitate mounting.

He then bolted the box into place, using standard 5/16-inch bolts with nuts and lock washers.

We now have a super storage compartment that can be secured with a padlock.

Installing the Fuel Tank

Mount It Out Of Harm's Way

Earlier in this book, we presented several variations of fuel tanks, everything from a 10-gallon beer keg to a racing type fuel cell. For the project dune buggy, I opted to use a spun aluminum fuel tank that holds 11 gallons. The installation of our fuel tank was less of a challenge than the storage box in that only one additional brace had to be made.

We started by first installing one of our trusty Coleman clamps on each side of the buggy frame rail just behind the storage box. NOTE: For safety's sake, always mount a fuel tank inside the frame rail.

After electing to use an 11-gallon spun aluminum fuel tank, we determined that only a single additional brace had to be made. We started by installing one of our handy Coleman clamps on each side of the buggy frame rail just behind the storage box. NOTE: For safety reasons, always mount a fuel tank inside the frame rail.

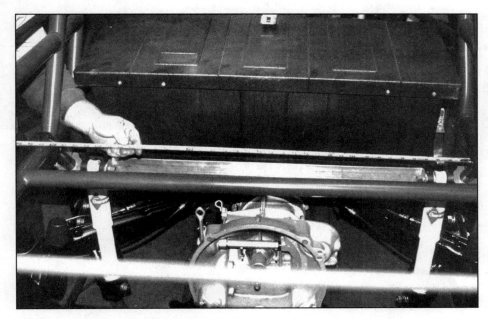

With the Coleman clamps secured, we measured the distance between the two clamps.

After calculating the length needed, we cut a piece of 1x1/8-inch aluminum stock to size, allowing two extra inches on each end for the 90-degree angle that would be bent at each end. We then made the 90-degree bends.

We drilled a 1/2-inch hole in each end and secured our brace to the Coleman clamps.

We then positioned the two fuel tank straps supplied with the new fuel tank on top of the brace we had just made and on the dune buggy frame support. We then positioned the two tank straps so that they were an equal distance from each side of the outside frame rail.

Our tank strap locations were calculated and we then marked them. We drilled our holes in both mounting braces.

With the Coleman clamps on and secured, we measured the distance between the two clamps and, after calculating the length needed, we cut a piece of 1x1/8-inch aluminum stock and allowed two inches extra on each end for the 90-degree angle that would be bent on each end. After making the bends, we drilled a 1/2-inch hole in each end and secured our brace to the Coleman clamps. We then positioned the pair of fuel tank straps on top of the brace we had just made and on the dune buggy frame support. We then positioned the two straps so they were an equal distance

from each side of the outside frame rail. Our tank strap locations were calculated, after which we marked, drilled, and bolted the straps into position.

Most fuel tanks come with a threaded fitting in the bottom for the installation of a fuel hose nipple, and ours was no exception. We chose a fuel shut-off valve similar to those used on ATVs or motorcycles. To install any fuel hose nipple or shut-off valve, be sure to use Teflon tape on the threads to guard against fuel leaks. Then insert the shut-off valve in the tank and tighten it securely.

The fuel tank was then placed inside the fuel tank straps. It was necessary to slightly bend the straps outward to accomplish this. With the tank in place and centered, it is now a simple task of putting the strap bolts into place and tightening them up. The new fuel tank is now securely mounted and ready for its first fill-up.

NOTE: Spun aluminum fuel tanks come with either a center fill neck or a side fill neck. My past experience has been that a side fill is much easier to reach when fueling up. ∎

Next, we bolted the straps into position.

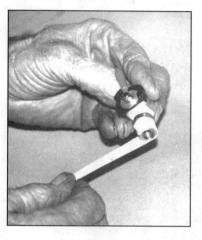

Most fuel tanks come with a threaded fitting in the bottom for installation of a fuel hose nipple, and ours was no exception. We chose a fuel shut-off valve similar to those used on ATVs or motorcycles. To install any fuel hose nipple or shut-off valve be sure to use Teflon tape on the threads to guard against fuel leaks.

We then inserted the shut-off valve in our tank and tightened securely.

The fuel tank was then inserted inside the fuel tank straps. It was necessary to slightly bend the straps outward so they would accept the tank.

With the tank in place and centered, it is now a simple task of putting the strap bolts into place and tightening them down.

Our new fuel tank now rests safely inside the frame rails.

Selecting and Installing Seats

Safety, Comfort and Appearance

When your friends are dismounting their buggies and complaining bitterly about their numb posteriors, you'll be glad you invested a little extra time and thought in the selection of your seats. If you choose better seats with the proper padding and covers, you certainly won't regret it.

Seats do play an all-important role in the comfort and safety of any dune buggy. Choose them wisely. I have personally made my own blunders in this area, so listen to someone who's been there and done that! First, determine where and how you will be driving your buggy. For instance, do you intend to drive moderate trails and dirt or gravel roads, or will you build a show buggy that's driven only on paved highways, or possibly a race-only monster that spends its entire life kicking serious dirt? Whatever the case, the first priority is always safety, followed by comfort and then appearance.

With safety considerations first and foremost, choose a sturdy unit that can be securely mounted to either the frame rails or the floor pan. This rule applies to all seats regardless of the type or design. Race-only seats require super construction and strength and are made to wrap around and fit the driver and/or passenger perfectly and to

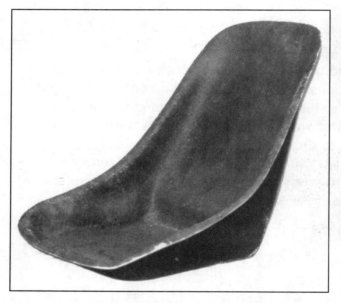

Comfort, safety and appearance are all important factors in selecting the seats for a dune buggy. Since my buggy was going to be built for street and moderate off-road use, such as dirt, rock and semi-rough terrain, I ruled out the lighter-weight fiberglass seat, which is usually used in low-budget street buggies and is not recommended for off-road use.

allow no movement of the occupants when blasting through turns or vaulting over jumps. CAUTION: All seats require approved seat belts to ensure safety.

The next consideration is comfort. No matter what type of seat you choose make sure padded seat covers are available for that specific design, as seats come in many sizes and shapes. After you have located proper covers ask about additional preformed tush padding. If they don't have it, make your own by cutting sections out of carpet padding, or go to the local variety store and pur-

chase a section of foam rubber; the thick rubber outdoor sleeping mats work great.

Finally, there is appearance. When doing a basic buggy, what's wrong with a sturdy basic seat? Absolutely nothing ... they are inexpensive and with proper padding work very well. Maybe it's a show winner you intend to build; if so, spend the extra money and get the best of all worlds in a very sturdy, very sleek seat with the classiest of covers. Building a show winner demands extra time, effort and, naturally, more money.

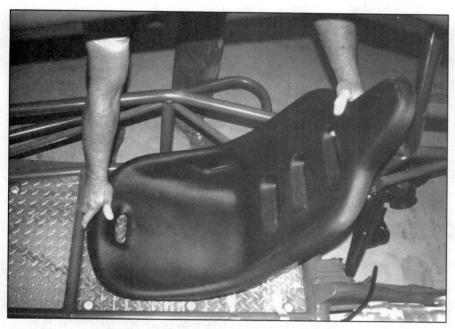

I chose a molded plastic type of seat, which is very sturdy and with proper cushioning and available seat covers, quite comfortable for extended traveling or bouncing around on rough terrain. First we positioned the seats on the dune buggy floor pan to determine the most advantageous mounting position, remembering that I wanted to use adjustable seat tracks on the driver's side and a solid mount seat on the passenger side.

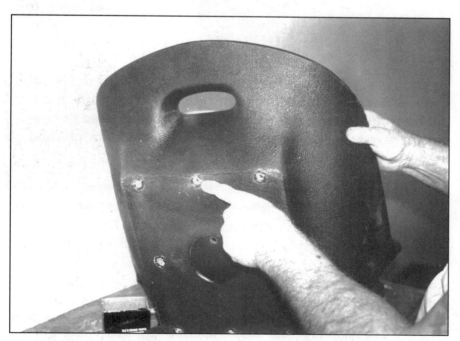

To install the molded seats into the project dune buggy it was necessary to fabricate a flat metal plate that would mount to the bottom of the seat. There are mounting threads molded into the seat itself.

Considering our intended usage, we selected the molded plastic type, which is very sturdy. And with proper cushioning and available seat covers, this seat is quite comfortable for extended traveling or when bouncing around on rough terrain.

On the dune buggies I have built in the past, I have incorporated adjustable seat tracks on the driver's side and a solid mount seat on the passenger side. The reasons for the adjustable driver's seat are obvious ... everyone is not built the same and comfort is essential for good safe driving, especially when you are doing some off roading. There is ample leg room on the passenger side since there are no pedals to interfere with your riding comfort, so an adjustable seat is not necessary on the right side. My primary supplier, Larry's Off Road Center, Dayton, Ohio, had an ample supply of the adjustable seat tracks in stock. If you are unable to find them locally, they can be mail-ordered from national shops like Larry's, which ship all over the continent, as well as overseas.

To install the seats it was necessary to fabricate a flat metal plate that would mount to the bottom of the seat. There are mounting threads molded into the seat itself, so we measured across the bottom of the seat allowing a one-inch overlap beyond the outside of the threaded holes. We then went to a local metal fabrication shop and had two metal plates cut to our dimensions.

We then found the proper locations for drilling our mounting holes in the plates by putting a dab of white grease around each threaded hole in the seat bottom and gently placing the metal plate squarely on the seat bottom and pressing down. What this did was transfer the white grease around the threaded holes to the metal plate. We then turned the plate over to expose the grease spots; those were the locations for drilling the mounting holes.

With all the mounting holes drilled, we installed bolts, flat washers and lock washers through the metal plate into the seats' threaded

After we had two metal plates cut to our specs, we found the proper locations for drilling our mounting holes in the plates by putting a dab of white grease around each threaded hole in the seat bottom and then gently placing the metal plate squarely on the seat bottom and pressing down. This forced the white grease around the threaded holes and onto the metal plate. By turning the plates over, we exposed the grease spots and those were the locations for drilling the mounting holes.

With all the mounting holes drilled, we installed bolts, flat washers and lock washers through the metal plate into the seats' threaded holes.

holes. We then tightened the bolts securely. After we had the metal plate secured to the seat bottom we then repositioned the seats in their desired location on the dune buggy floor pan. Be sure to do this with both seats. When we had both seats positioned we marked these locations by drawing an outline on the floor pan with a marking pen around the entire outside diameter of the square metal seat plate.

We removed both seats, after which we removed the seat plates from the bottoms of the seats. We then repositioned the passenger seat plate in the previously marked location on the floor pan. While holding the seat plate in position, we drilled a 3/8-inch hole in each corner of the seat plate and through the floor pan to secure the plate to the floor pan.

We then mounted our adjustable seat tracks on the driver's side in the previously marked area on the floor

We then tightened the bolts securely. After we had the metal plate secured to the seat bottom, we then repositioned the seats in their desired location on the dune buggy floor pan. Do this with both seats. Then mark these locations by drawing an outline on the floor pan with a marking pen around the entire outside diameter of the square metal seat plate. Then remove both seats and unbolt the seat plates from the seat bottoms and reposition the passenger seat plate in the previously marked location on the floor pan.

While holding the seat plate in position, drill a 3/8-inch hole in each corner of the seat plate and through the floor pan to secure the plate to the floor pan.

Then we mounted our adjustable seat tracks on the driver's side in the previously marked area on the floor pan. After carefully placing the seat plate on the four studs in the adjustable seat tracks, we marked their locations on the bottom of the seat plate.

pan. After carefully placing the seat plate on the four studs in the adjustable seat tracks, we marked their location on the bottom of the seat plate. We then drilled the four 5/16-inch holes that will be necessary for mounting the seat plate to the adjustable seat tracks. We then took the driver's side seat plate and reinstalled it on the bottom of the left seat. Next, we took the passenger's side seat plate and reinstalled it to the bottom of the passenger seat.

Now that all of our seat mounting holes have been located and drilled, and our seat plates have been installed on the seat bottoms, we can install our seats at any time. But permanent seat installation will be delayed until the very end of the building process. The reason for this is that the installed seats will be in the way, interfering with the installation of wiring, clutch tube, accelerator tube, shifter box, etc. It's okay, of course, to temporarily install both seats for the purposes of determining shifter, clutch, brake, and steering wheel location. When it's time to permanently install the seats, be sure to use all mounting holes. Also, use only industrial-grade bolts, nuts and lock washers.

When we permanently install the seats near the end of the assembly process, we'll also install the seat belts and seat covers. ∎

We then drilled the four 5/16-inch holes necessary for mounting the seat plate to the adjustable seat tracks. We then took the driver's side seat plate and reinstalled it on the bottom of the left seat and the passenger's side seat plate and reinstalled it to the bottom of the passenger seat. Now that all of the seat mounting holes have been located and drilled, and the seat plates installed on the seat bottoms, we can install our seats at any time, preferably at the end of the project so they don't interfere with other work on the buggy.

Selecting and Installing Seat Belts

A Matter of Personal Safety ... and Possibly Survival

Accidents can happen, and when a mishap occurs while driving or riding in your dune buggy, at that precise instant your best friend will be your seat belt. But it must be a quality belt, properly installed and, most importantly, in use! Even a seat belt — probably the greatest single safety advance in the history of motorized travel — is totally useless if it's not buckled up.

Seat belts come in a variety of designs, widths, colors and prices, but their main purpose is to help prevent injury and even death in the event of an accident. Don't even think about building or driving a buggy without a quality set of seat belts. And that warning applies to operation on and off the road, even at home in your driveway.

At the bottom end of the scale would be the single lap belt, which consists of a two-inch wide belt that bolts to the floor pan. It features a basic latch and is designed to keep the occupant restrained in the seat. (I have never installed or used this type in a dune buggy and personally would not recommend them.)

The next step up is the two-inch

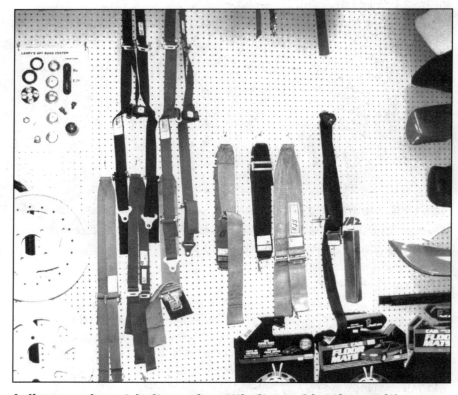

I discussed seat belts and seat-belt combinations with Charles White of Larry's Off Road Center, Dayton, Ohio, and he showed me these restraint systems, just a few of the seat belts and options available.

Since the project buggy would be driven on the street and in moderate off-road use, such as on dirt or gravel roads and off-road trails, the two-inch wide lap and shoulder harness combination was recommended. And that's what I bought, in red to match the buggy's finish. One complete set is required per seat.

To install the belts, Bob Supinger started by mounting a Coleman clamp on the frame bar located behind the driver's seat and, with a 1/2-inch industrial strength bolt and lock washer, installed the shoulder harness set to the Coleman clamp.

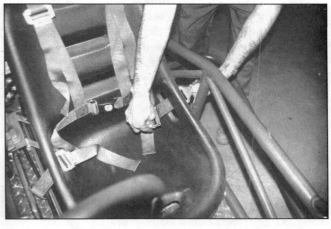

Then he tightened it securely in place.

Next, Bob positions the lap belts thru the pre-formed slots in the bucket seats.

wide lap belt combined with a two-inch wide shoulder harness with a basic latch. This harness system not only keeps the occupant strapped down in the seat, but also keeps the upper body from going forward in the event of a head-on collision with another vehicle, a tree, a huge boulder, etc. This combination is probably the restraint system of choice when building the average dune buggy, both in quality, safety, and price.

Moving further up the scale of safety performance and features, you will find a three-inch lap belt with

two-inch shoulder harnesses. This combination comes with a heavy-duty latch. To move up another step in quality and safety, consider this combination: three-inch lap belts with three-inch shoulder belts, also with the heavy-duty latch. If you are considering any serious off-road activity, by all means opt to use this type of belt system.

Should you want to really mix it up in all-out off-road racing, the only choice is three-inch lap belts with three-inch shoulder belts, plus a fifth belt called a sub belt. And even with this super strong belt system, other

safety features are required for racing. Among them are: shoulder and neck pads and braces; approved fire or driving suits; window nets; limit straps for arms and legs; approved fireproof gloves; and driving shoes. The more safety equipment you have on your buggy and on your person, the more protection you have from injury, and worse!

Any of the aforementioned seat-belt combinations can be ordered specifically for mounting on the roll bar or floor pan. ∎

Then he checks for a proper mounting location on the floor pan. Fortunately, when he positioned the lap belts on the floor pan, the welded-on floor tabs proved to be in a perfect location for mounting. This was almost too easy; no holes to drill, no mounting brackets to manufacture, etc.

The installation was as simple as unscrewing the floor pan retaining bolts on both sides of the seat, substituting industrial strength bolts with flat washers and lock washers in their place, and then reinstalling the new bolts thru the welded-on tab and the floor pan with the seat belt mounting bracket attached. After both sides were bolted down, Bob tightened everything down.

Bob then positions himself squarely in the driver's seat and proceeds to adjust the lap belt for a proper fit. It should run across the pelvic area.

He then fine adjusted the shoulder harness to produce a snug but comfortable fit. To work properly, the belts must fit snugly.

Finally, with the seat in its proper location and the belts adjusted correctly, we now have a seat belt system that is ready to perform to manufacturer specs.

Assembling the Generator/Fan Shroud

Life and Death for a Bug Engine

The engine that was rebuilt for the dune buggy project was a 1600 VW Bug engine. This is an air-cooled engine that uses no radiator or water-based coolant of any kind to keep it alive and well, thus the generator/fan shroud assembly is essentially the difference between life and death for the engine.

Obviously, this is one area that requires special attention and care. With the unique design and strategic location of this powerful little dynamo, the sheer volume and force of air that it produces is like a mini hurricane. The simplicity of the unit is such that with the assembly mounted in place directly over the cylinder heads, the shroud is positioned so that both cylinder heads receive equal amounts of air flow.

When mounted and operational, the crank pulley turns the fan/generator belt, which in turn drives the generator output shaft. That shaft has a fan blade connected at the opposite end from the fan belt. Not only does this turning of the fan blade produce sufficient air for proper cooling of the engine, this same movement of the generator shaft combined with the internal workings of the generator produces D/C voltage that keeps the

A generator/fan shroud assembly consists of these basic parts (from left): Fan shroud; locking nut and wave washer; fan alignment hub; spacing shims; fan; inner fan cover; generator and related hardware; reinforcement ring; and the outer fan cover.

Bob Supinger starts by positioning a new Bosch 12-volt generator so that the ground strap hole is pointing in the up position and both generator wire terminals are located to the right as indicated.

With the generator properly positioned, Supie installs the outer fan cover over the generator studs.

Next comes the reinforcement ring with the concave side down.

Finally the inner fan cover is installed over the generator studs. Caution: If this last cover is improperly installed, it will cause overheating of the generator and premature failure.

When installing the inner generator cover, make sure the slot (arrow) in the cover is pointing in the down position, or opposite the generator ground strap hole.

After both generator covers and the reinforcement ring are in place, Supie puts a small amount of Loctite retaining compound on the generator stud threads.

battery fully charged. The battery, in turn, powers the ignition, lights and all the accessories necessary for operating the vehicle.

We chose for the project buggy a new Bosch 12-volt generator. Again, a rebuilt unit is also a good deal. But, should a used unit better fit your budget, it's to your advantage to have it tested before installing it on the engine. Most starter and alternator rebuild shops can do this for you.

However, if you do not have access to a test facility, you can use a 12-volt battery to test a used generator yourself. While being very careful not to create sparks, and wearing safety glasses, hook one end of a set

He then installs the flat washers and nuts.

Using a 10-mm wrench, Supie tightens them securely. Caution: Again check the inner cover slot for proper position.

Supie now places the Woodruff key in the slot on the generator output shaft.

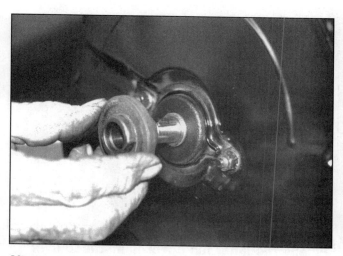

Next comes the fan alignment hub.

of jumper cables to a 12-volt battery, verifying positive and negative, then ground the negative cable to the generator case. Now touch the positive cable to the DF or field terminal on the generator (DF will be clearly marked on the generator housing). If the output shaft on the generator turns (or motors), it's a good indication that the unit is in working condition.

Note: This is not a chiseled-in-stone guarantee of a perfect unit, but in most cases this test is fairly accurate. Before deciding to install the used generator, inspect it for frayed wiring, plus check the brushes, this can be done by looking inside the generator thru the slots in the gener-

ator housing. If the generator does need brushes, now is the time to install them, because after the unit is on the engine the bottom brush is difficult to change (see the "Generator brush replacement" chapter.)

The fan shroud we used was a new chrome-plated unit designed to fit the offset oil cooler that we would install on our engine (see the "Engine" Chapter.) Fan shrouds come in many shapes and sizes, so check with your parts supplier for the one that fits your particular needs, whether it be for a stock engine, high-performance engine, stock oil cooler, external oil cooler, etc. There is even the option of using a fan shroud with air outlet tubes, so that with the addi-

tion of exhaust heat exchangers you could have heat in a full-bodied dune buggy.

Our generator and fan shroud assembly consists of these basic components:

- Generator
- Woodruff key
- Outer fan cover
- Reinforcement ring
- Inner fan cover
- Fan alignment hub
- Fan blade
- Spacing shims
- Locking washer
- Special nut

The unit can be assembled at any time during the buggy-building pro-

With the alignment hub in place, Supie installs the two hub shims.

He then installs the fan blade.

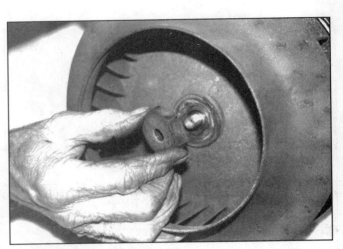

Final installation of the parts concludes with the large washer (left) and special nut (right). Caution: Make sure the slot in the washer aligns with the slot in the hub before the nut is installed.

ject. Our unit was installed on the engine during the final stages of the engine rebuild.

Caution: When the fan unit has been installed and the engine is running, never get near or place your hands near the fan blade. When operating, this fan creates a powerful vacuum force at the rear opening in the fan shroud that is capable of pulling anything, including one's hands, into the fan blade, with the potential of causing serious injury, or worse. Some aftermarket fan shrouds are designed to accept a screened guard over the shroud opening to help prevent anything from being sucked into the blade. It's definitely a recommended safety feature wherever feasible. ■

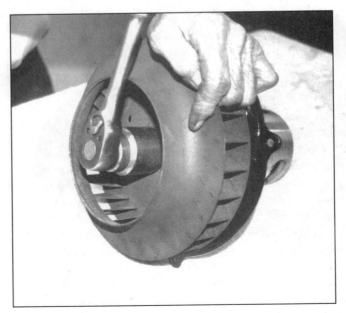

Supie now uses a 36-mm socket and 1/2-inch-drive ratchet to secure the special nut.

The fan shroud is then placed on top of two short pieces of 2x4 lumber with the back side of the shroud facing down and the 2x4's positioned to expose the entire circumference of the hole.

The nut was then torqued to 44 lbs.-ft.

Before the final installation of the generator and fan unit on the new fan shroud, Supie inserts the generator/fan unit into the shroud and holds it in place while spinning the outer generator output shaft. If the fan blade is properly shimmed and everything is in order, the fan blade should not rub the fan shroud. Caution: If the fan blade does rub the shroud or fan cover, it will require disassembly of the generator/fan unit and the addition or extraction of shims as necessary. And, don't forget to retorque that large special nut.

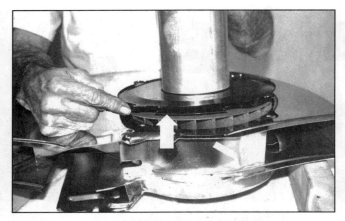

There were no rubbing noises, so one final inspection was made to ensure that the slot in the fan cover pointed to the bottom of the fan shroud (arrow), and that the generator ground strap hole pointed up.

He then installed the four cover retaining bolts.

Next, Supie tightened the retaining bolts securely.

Bob Supinger examines the completely assembled generator/fan shroud assembly. The fully functional and good looking engine cooling and charging unit is now ready to be installed on the engine.

Replacing Generator Brushes

A Re-volting Project

You can't beat a brand new generator, fresh from the factory, or, almost as good, a newly rebuilt generator. Neither would need any work and both would come ready to install. Rebuilt units usually come with a full complement of new internal parts, including armature, field windings, and new brushes.

However, if you're living within a budget, as most hobbyists are, repairing your used generator may be a necessity. If you should elect to install a used generator on your project dune buggy, replacing the brushes in a VW Bug 12-volt generator is a relatively simple task. The only tools needed are a medium-size flat-blade screwdriver (preferably one with a magnetized tip), a screw holder, and a hook device, such as a small Allen wrench.

The painless way to do this is to have the unit on the work bench. Otherwise, when the generator is installed on the buggy it creates difficulty in replacing the lower brush since the brush is very tough to access when you are attempting to replace it while it's pointing down. To complicate things even further, you have limited visibility. When the generator is installed on the buggy,

A brand new generator, such as this Bosch unit, is ideal if the budget permits. Or a factory rebuilt unit is also a good bet. In either case, all one has to do is buy it and install it.

there are two ways to replace the lower brush, just feel your way through it, or stand on your head and attempt the job. (CAUTION: I don't recommend standing on your head to do it.)

Follow the steps illustrated here and your used generator will be charging your battery at peak levels

once again; assuming, of course, that your generator's armature and field windings are in good condition. If they're bad, you'll need to take the unit to a professional shop for a complete overhaul. Procedures for testing a generator for a bad armature or field windings are outlined in the "Generator-fan shroud" chapter. ∎

Most used generators you'll find will at least need new brushes, and installing them is no big deal. With the used generator on the work bench and either one of the two openings in the unit facing up, Bill Fast inserts the flat-blade screwdriver in the screw that holds the brush lead to the bracket. (CAUTION: When removing this screw it's very easy to drop the screw or washer into the generator, so be careful.)

He then backs the screw out and removes it. With the screw out of the way he takes a hook device, such as a small Allen wrench, and inserts it into the brush tension spring and gently pulls back to release the brush. It is not necessary to remove this tension spring.

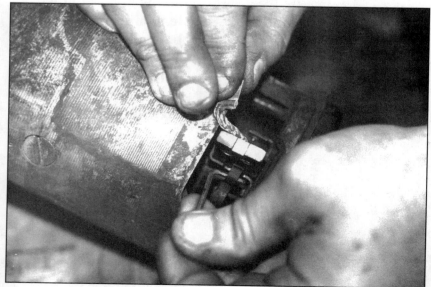

After the tension spring is sufficiently far enough away from the brush, Bill removes the brush from its holder. While keeping the tension spring held away from the brush holder, he installs the new brush by simply inserting it into the holder and pushing it inward.

Fast now gently releases the spring to let it rest on the new brush.

With the new brush in place, he inserts the brush lead retaining screw into the screw-holding device.

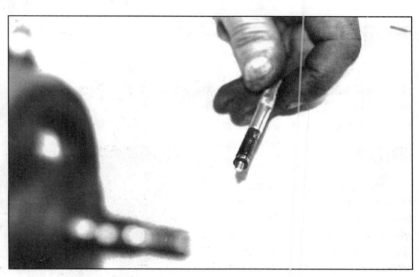

He then uses the screw holder to re-install the screw and the brush lead into the threaded bracket and finishes the job by using the screwdriver to tighten it. Bill has now completed the installation of one of the two generator brushes, so the next step is to turn the generator over and repeat the same procedure with the other brush.

Disassembling, Rebuilding and Reassembling the Engine

Breathing New Life into a VW Bug Mill

The heart of any motorized vehicle is the component that makes it "motorized" — the engine. Without a strong heartbeat, a buggy is just another conglomeration of metal, plastic and rubber. Power for a dune buggy can come from the unlikeliest of sources — a Chevy small block V-8, a Ford V-6, or a Chrysler four-banger — but the vast majority of dune buggies rely on one of the world's most dependable, economical and serviceable engines ... the Volkswagen Bug four-cylinder air-cooled powerplant that earned a reputation for toughness and durability beyond all reasonable expectations.

And, since the VW Bug broke the Ford Model T's record for longevity and production, there exists an ample supply of the sturdy little engines throughout the world. In fact, in some countries, you can still buy a new VW Bug engine.

For the project dune buggy we salvaged a used VW Bug 1600 dual-port engine.

For our project dune buggy, we salvaged a stock 1600 VW engine out of a 1973 Bug with the intentions of rebuilding it so that it would once again perform and look like new. The next thing that was needed was a VW shop manual that covered air-cooled VW Bugs. Since our project engine and tranny came out of a 1973 Bug, a manual that covered from 1968 to 1973 sufficed. The manual was used for such information as detailed schematics of engine components and torque specifications for all aspects of the engine and transmission, as well as torsion arms, wheel bearings, front and rear suspensions, and brake mounting hardware. These valuable books of knowledge can be purchased at any dune buggy supply store, numerous book stores, and even many libraries.

Bob Supinger started the engine disassembly by removing the alternator belt and pulleys. A flat-blade screwdriver was inserted in the slot that is in the rear alternator pulley and was lodged against one of the bolts that holds the generator together. Doing this prevents the pulley from turning so the retaining nut can be loosened and removed. Next, Bob took the same screwdriver and removed the screws that hold the engine covers in place. There were a number of these covers mounted on the engine, and he removed all of them that he had access to, including the rear cover and front cover, along with any additional screws that were exposed at the time. The main purpose when disassembling a VW Bug engine is to strip it down to the basic block as easily and quickly as possible. This is not a clean project, so it's a good idea to wear old clothes, and gloves. Eye protection isn't a bad idea either.

Removing exhaust nuts can sometimes be tough because they are prone to rust seizure, but with a little help from a propane torch and patience, the job can be handled. CAUTION: Do not have any flammable materials or batteries in the area when using a torch, even a small one. After Bob had removed all of the exhaust and related parts, he then removed the rest of the retaining screws, plus the alternator strap, and carefully lifted the fan shroud assembly up and off the engine.

The engine oil cooler was now exposed. This old oil cooler was very clean and dry, indicating no leaks, so it would be cleaned and reused on the rebuilt engine. Bob then directed his attention to the removal of the clutch and pressure plate. This required taking the retaining bolts out and carefully lifting the clutch away from the flywheel. Take note here as to how the clutch disc is installed; the flat side should face the flywheel.

Next came the removal of the flywheel. CAUTION: This unit is quite heavy and is adorned with sharp teeth on the ring gear, so be extra careful when removing it from the crankshaft. To remove the gland nut that holds it on the crank requires the use of an air impact gun and a 36-mm impact socket.

After the flywheel was off and safely on the work bench, Bob then pried the old crank (or flywheel) seal out of the engine case. This gave him access to the three adjustment shims that will be reused on the new engine. With most of the heavyweight parts off the engine, Bob and an assistant mounted the remaining engine case and related parts onto a portable engine stand.

Now all the extra parts such as the fuel pump, alternator stand, oil cooler, oil pump, valve covers, valve rockers, push rods, cylinder heads, push rod tubes, cylinders, pistons and the old oil sending unit could be stripped from the block. When all this was gone, what was left was a block, crankshaft, and rods. Do not attempt to disassemble the two case halves without removing the oil pump first.

With the engine block stripped Bob removed all case nuts and bolts. Be aware that some of the case nuts could be hidden in years of caked-on dirt and grime, so search them out diligently. Bob then split the case by inserting a screwdriver between the two case halves and prying the two sections apart. After the case was apart it provided access to the old crankshaft (which would be inspected and reused).

He then removed the crank with the rods attached, and then liberated the camshaft, valve lifters and all the old bearings, being extra careful not to lose any of the engine bearing guide pins. Finally, Bob removed the distributor gear and shims. Don't lose these shims either; they will be reused in the new engine.

Cleaning of the case can be a real chore, but it must be done. Donning his safety glasses, Bob set to the project at hand. After it was spotless, Bob, still wearing his safety glasses, took an air hose and used compressed air to blow out every nook and cranny of both case halves.

At this point, the reassembly of the engine was about to begin. To start, Bob took the case half with the six large studs in it and mounted it on the engine stand. He then installed six new O-ring case stud seals. After installing the bearing alignment pins that had been salvaged from the old engine, Bob installed all the engine bearings. He then had the crankshaft checked with a micrometer for proper size bearings, and had the front cam gear and distributor gear removed to provide access to the old front bearing. After removal of the old bearing, a new one was inserted in its place. With the new bearing installed the cam and distributor gears were then pressed back on.

Removal of the front cam gear and the distributor gear are jobs best left to a local machine shop, unless you have the proper pullers and the experience to use them correctly. The distributor gear is made of brass and can be damaged easily.

After the crank assembly was complete, Bob then reinstalled the crank assembly, the camshaft and lifters, the distributor gear and shims. He then put a light coating of Permatex aviation sealer on the case sealing surface and the rear cam plug before reassembling both case halves together and installing all the case

nuts and bolts, and tightening them to specs.

Now with the basic block assembled, Bob installed all the new pistons and cylinders, push-rod tubes, cylinder heads, the valve system, the oil pump, the crank pulley, the generator stand (we opted to use a generator instead of an alternator), distributor drive gear and washers, distributor drive, fuel pump, new oil cooler seals, and oil cooler. The flywheel and seals were the next order of business. Before installing the flywheel seal Bob first set the crank endplay by checking the run-out with a dial indicator. The book called for an .008" tolerance. With this done he then installed the flywheel seal and shims, (there must be three shims), after which the new gland nut was torqued to specs. Then the clutch system was installed.

Bob then proceeded with such items as adjusting the valves, installing the oil sending unit, replacing the spark plugs, mounting the super shiny chrome cylinder head covers, installing the generator and fan belt, etc.

The intake manifold and the exhaust system were next on the list, followed shortly by the carburetor, which Bob had rebuilt with a new kit. Bob then installed the clutch throw-out bearing on the transmission.

Next, Bob installed what would turn out to be one of his best rebuilt engines, and he's rebuilt hundreds of them over the years. When the dune buggy had been completely wired and all the engine electrical components hooked up, the engine cranked over approximately 10 revolutions before firing to life. From that point on, it was simply a matter of setting everything to spec and doing a little fine tuning. ∎

Engine Disassembly

Bob Supinger started the disassembly by putting a flat-blade screwdriver in the upper slot of the alternator pulley and, using a 21-mm wrench, he removed the retaining nut, front alternator pulley, and the alternator belt.

Then using a flat-blade screwdriver he removed the retaining screws for the rear engine cover.

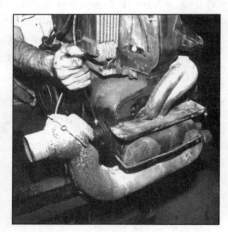

This afforded Bob easy access to the rear exhaust nuts on one of the old heat exchangers. These units will not be re-used on the rebuilt engine.

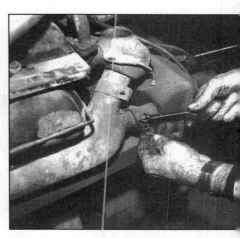

Here Bob removes the distributor (arrow). This was done by removing a single hold down nut with a 13-mm wrench, and pulling the distributor up and out of the engine block.

With the distributor out of the way, he proceeded with the removal of some exhaust nuts and bolts.

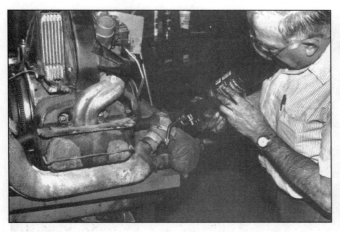

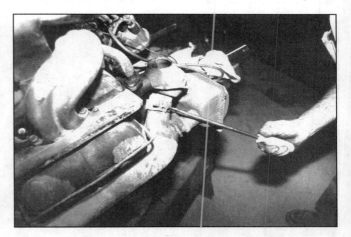

When loosening exhaust nuts and bolts, Bob found it necessary to use a propane torch to add a little heat for easier disassembly. Caution: Do not have any flammable material or batteries in the area when using any type of torch.

Bob then removed these band clamps, which help secure the heat exchangers to part of the muffler system.

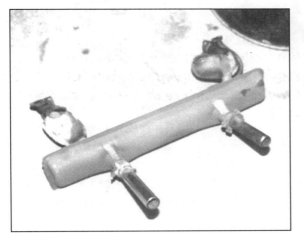

With all the exhaust nuts out of the way, the old muffler could then be removed and disposed of properly.

Bob can now finish the removal of both the right and left heat exchangers.

After removal of the two screws that go thru both cylinder head covers and into the stock fan shroud, Bob removed the nut and bolt that goes thru the alternator retaining strap. This metal strap keeps the alternator in place.

With the alternator strap and bolt removed, Bob then carefully lifted the fan shroud and alternator up and off the engine.

Bob next removed the two retaining nuts that secure the intake manifold to the cylinder head. There are two nuts and one intake manifold on each cylinder head.

With all four intake manifold nuts removed, plus one center nut, Bob lifted the complete unit free from the engine.

To remove the clutch disc and pressure plate, Bob removed the six retaining bolts and washers, which allowed the disc and plate to separate from the flywheel.

Take note as to how the plate and disc come out of the flywheel, it will help when it comes time to re-install a new one on the rebuilt engine. The flat side of the disc (arrow) faces the flywheel.

To remove the gland nut that holds the flywheel to the crankshaft required the use of an air-operated impact gun. This 36-mm nut must be super tight, so removing one is no easy task.

With the gland nut removed Bob carefully used a pry bar to separate the flywheel from the crankshaft. Caution: Be extremely careful here, these flywheels are very heavy, and the starter ring gear that is attached to it has sharp teeth.

Having removed the flywheel, Bob used the same pry bar to remove the rear crankshaft seal.

After removal of the old crank seal, he now had access to the three shims that would be used to reset the crankshaft end play in the rebuilt engine.

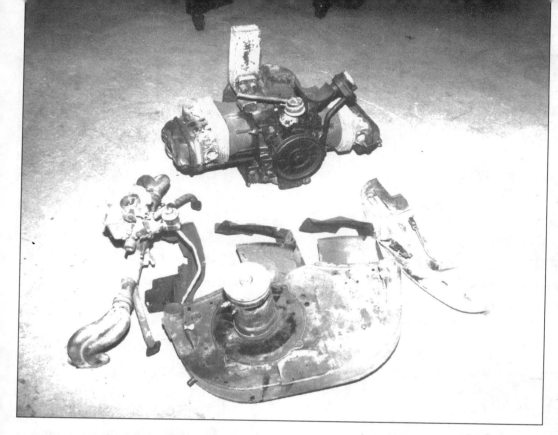

Bob had removed the engine parts that add excessive weight, such as clutch and disc, flywheel, alternator and shroud, and all exhaust related parts.

With the engine secure on the stand, Bob removed the crank bolt and the lower crank pulley.

Then, with some assistance from friend Jeff Grimes, Bob lifted the engine onto the engine stand and bolted it into place.

The fuel pump retaining nuts had been removed and the fuel pump and rod had been set aside, so the next order of business was the removal of the fuel pump flange.

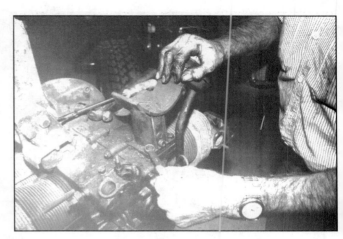

To remove the alternator stand Bob started by loosening and removing the four retaining nuts.

He then carefully lifted the stand up and away from the engine.

To remove the oil cooler Bob started by removing the three retaining nuts that secure it to the engine.

Having removed the retaining nuts, Bob lifted the cooler away from the engine.

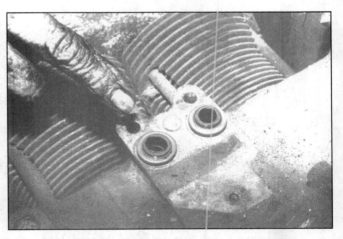

Bob points out that different engines use different oil cooler seals, so keep the old seals for comparison when installing new seals in the rebuilt engine.

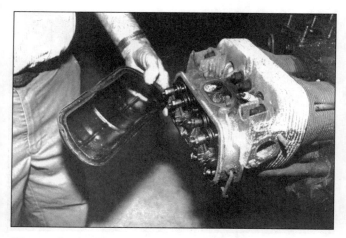

The valve covers on the salvage engine were held in place by a spring steel retaining bale. Bob used a screwdriver to release the bale, thus exposing the valves, valve rocker and push rods.

The next step was to take a 13-mm socket with a 3/8-inch ratchet, then remove the valve rocker retaining nuts and wave washers.

With the nuts loose Bob was then able to remove them by hand.

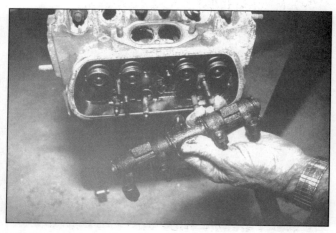

Next he removed the valve rocker shaft from the cylinder head.

After the valve rocker shaft was removed, Bob pulled the four push rods from the engine.

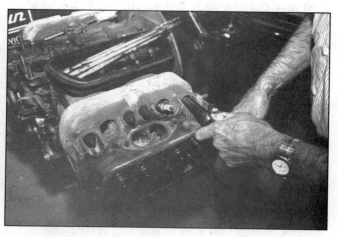

By using a 15-mm socket and 3/8-inch ratchet he now removed all cylinder head nuts and washers.

With all the cylinder head nuts out of the way, Bob carefully pulled the cylinder head away from the pistons and cylinders. This step also allowed the push-rod tubes to fall from the engine.

Bob then repeated the same procedure on the other side of the engine block.

On each set of cylinders there should be one air deflector. Bob removed these deflectors and put them aside to be used on the new piston and cylinder assemblies.

For the project buggy engine rebuild, we chose to use new pistons and cylinders, but if you intend to re-use the old pistons and cylinders with possibly a new set of rings be sure to mark the location of the cylinders, so they can be re-installed in their original location.

Next Bob started the removal of all four cylinders from the engine by grasping the cylinder and pulling outward.

With all four cylinders off and safely put to the side, Bob removed the old pistons from the connecting rods. Again, if the old pistons are to be re-used mark their cylinder location and put an arrow on each piston pointing toward the flywheel.

Using a pair of needle-nose pliers, Bob removed the two circlips from each of the four pistons. These clips keep the wristpins in place.

Using a hammer with a driver that is slightly smaller in diameter than the wristpin, Bob drove the four pins out of the pistons.

Bob used a 10-mm socket and 3/8-inch ratchet to remove the oil drain cover.

After removal of the oil drain cover, Bob found more evidence that this engine was in dire need of a rebuild.

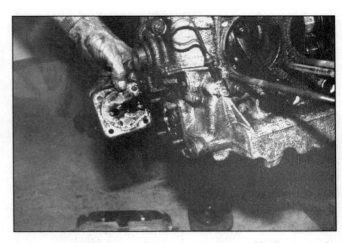

Removing the oil pump from the engine required the removal of the four retaining nuts that hold the pump cover.

After pulling the oil pump cover off the used oil pump, Bob found the oil pump and oil pump cover packed with sludge, a clear sign of poor maintenance.

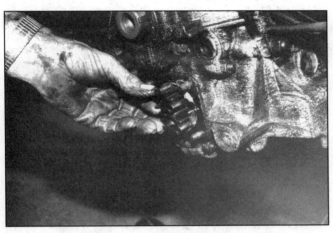

With the pump cover off, it was then a simple matter of pulling both pump gears out of the pump housing. This old pump will be discarded. Never use a worn oil pump in a fresh engine.

Now that the internal oil pump gears were out, Bob inserted a flat blade screwdriver between the oil pump housing and the block and with a hammer carefully tapped the screwdriver inward to separate the pump housing from the block.

The old pump can be rather tight in the block, but with persistence and careful prying with a screwdriver, the old pump is dislodged and can be tossed. Caution: When prying, be careful not to score or gouge the engine block.

Finally the block has been stripped to the point that Bob can now take a 13-mm and 17-mm sockets with a 3/8-inch drive ratchet and extension and start removing the upper and lower case nuts, bolts and washers. If an engine block has been fitted with self-sealing nuts, a 19-mm socket will be required.

Bob now had all case nuts and washers removed (check closely and don't miss any that might be covered with years of sludge and grime build-up). So, the next step was to insert a flat-blade screwdriver between the two case halves, and carefully pry them apart.

With the engine case (or block) pried apart, Bob rotated the engine on the stand, and then lifted the right side case half up and away from the left side as seen here.

With the two case halves separated, the next order of business was to remove the camshaft.

Then came the valve lifters.

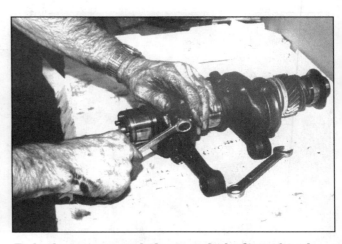

Bob then removed the crankshaft and rods by grasping the two connecting rods that were pointing up, and then lifting the assembly up and out of the case. He then laid the unit on the workbench and began disassembly of the connecting rods by first removing the rod nuts with a 14-mm wrench.

After Bob removed each rod from the crank, he discarded the old rod bearings. These will be replaced with fresh new ones during the engine rebuild.

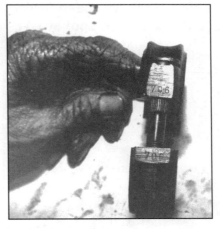

Bob made sure that all rod cap numbers corresponded with their matching rods.

With all rods removed Bob again verified rod caps with rods.

Here Bob taped the end of the crankshaft to avoid scoring the crank surface when removing the retainer ring for the distributor gear.

With a set of ring expander pliers Bob removed the retainer ring.

To access the front crank bearing, the cam gear must be removed. Here, Bob points to the cam gear, the removal of which requires a special puller. With the retaining ring out of the way, pulling the cam gear off also removes the distributor gear at the same time.

Bob had disassembled the crankshaft and now has it miked, cleaned and ready for reassembly. The next step was the removal of all the old engine bearings, such as the main bearings (above) and the cam bearings (below).

As indicated here, there are alignment pins in the block. These pins are visible with the old bearings removed. It is important that you remove these pins and put them in a safe place prior to cleaning the block. These pins will be re-used when the new bearings are installed.

When Bob had removed all the old bearings and pins, the last parts to come out were the distributor drive gear and shims.

Before re-assembly of the engine, Bob laid all the new replacement parts out on the work bench for visual inspection.

Half the engine block is sitting in a parts washer after receiving a thorough cleaning. The same treatment was given to all of the engine's parts.

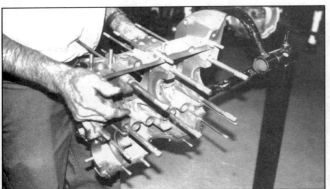

Bob Supinger securely mounted the side of the engine case with the six large studs to the engine stand.

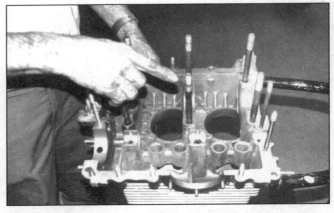

By attaching the case to the engine stand in this order, the six large case (or block) studs were sticking in the up position.

He then used an air nozzle to blow out all of the orifices and crevasses, making sure not to overlook any areas. Bob repeated this same air nozzle cleaning of the other engine half before assembling the two engine cases together. CAUTION: Wear safety glasses whenever using compressed air, but especially when blowing dirt, grime, etc., out of an engine block, or, in this instance, case halves.

After removing all six of the old case seals, Bob installed six new seals in the engine case.

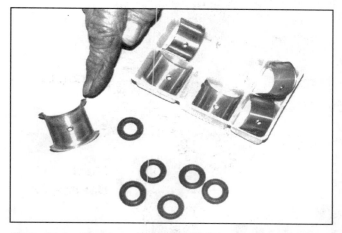

Now it was time to install the cam bearings in the case.

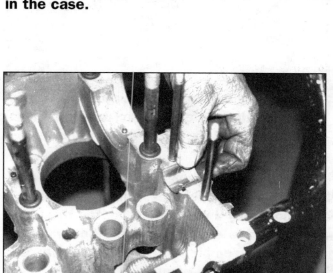

The narrowest bearing goes in the rear at the flywheel end of the case.

Next he installed the bearing alignment pins. There are four bearing alignment pins in the six stud case half, and one bearing alignment pin in the other case half and that will be installed later.

The bearing with the shoulder goes in the front or near the oil pump.

Bob made sure all bearing guides or notches aligned properly in the case half. We will assemble the remaining case half later on during assembly of the engine.

The front bearing alignment pin hole will point toward the flywheel end of the crank when properly installed on the crank.

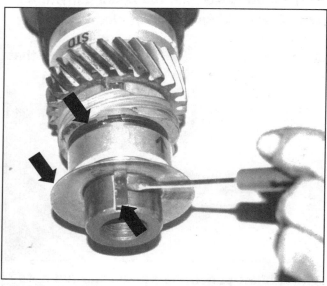

Bob then installed the number four crank bearing (top arrow) and oil slinger (lower left arrow) with the concave side of the slinger toward the flywheel end of the crank. Next he installed the crankshaft Woodruff key (lower right arrow) by lightly tapping it with a small hammer until seated.

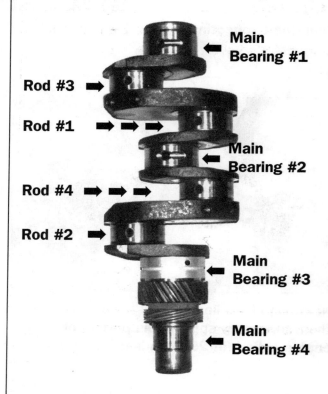

Main Bearing #1

Rod #3

Rod #1

Main Bearing #2

Rod #4

Rod #2

Main Bearing #3

Main Bearing #4

The crank should now be ready for the installation of the connecting rods as shown in this layout of the crankshaft.

Here Bob installs rod bearings in a rod cap.

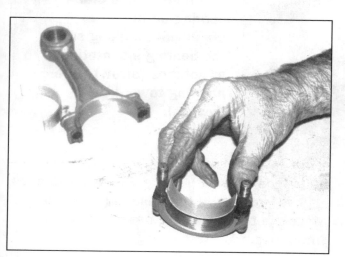

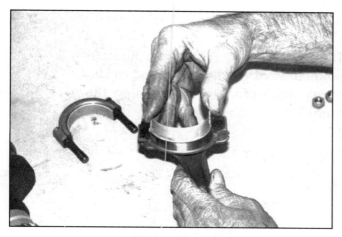

Then the connecting rod get its bearing.

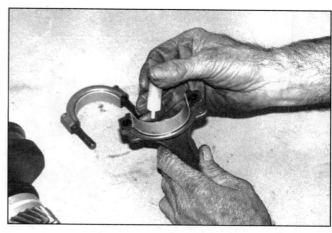

He then lubricated the rod bearings with an engine assembly lube.

Next, Bob installed the rod nuts and torqued them to factory specs. This particular engine called for 25 pounds-foot of torque.

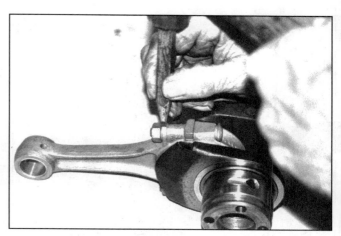

With a blunt punch, he staked the rod nuts in place and repeated this procedure for the remaining rods.

Bob then installed the rear number one crank bearing on the crankshaft, making sure the bearing indentations or notches (arrow) were pointing toward the flywheel.

He then installed the number two engine bearing in the case half (left), again making sure to lube all bearing surfaces (right).

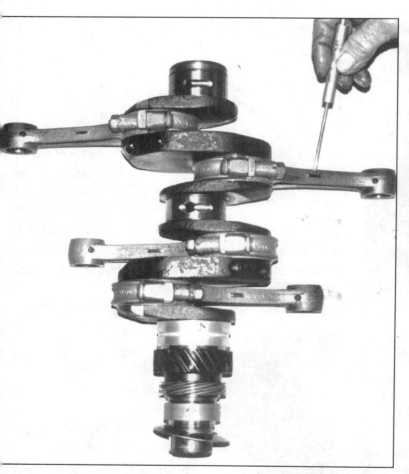

When viewing the crankshaft in this position with the rods in this order, Bob made sure all casting marks or forge marks, plus rod and cap numbers, were pointing in the up position. He then double checked to make sure he had all the crank bearings, and all the engine bearings in place and properly aligned.

With everything in order Bob then grasped the number one and two rods firmly, and lifted the completed crankshaft assembly above the engine case, which allowed the remaining number three and four rods to hang downward toward their respective positions in the center of number three and four cylinders. Bob then gently lowered the assembly into the engine case half, keeping all crank bearings properly aligned with their respective alignment pins.

When the crankshaft and bearings are in place, you should be able to set the number two crank bearing half on the crankshaft and there should be no movement or rocking of this bearing. If it rocks that means one or more of the other bearings are not in place on their guide pins.

It was necessary to slightly elevate the front of the crankshaft to install the camshaft and properly align the dot on the cam gear with the two dots on the crank gear.

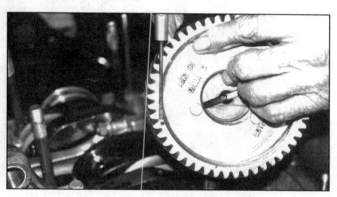

The single dot on the cam gear goes in the middle of the two dots on the crank gear.

This alignment is critical for proper valve timing. Double check this.

If the dots on the cam gear and crank gear are properly installed, the front crankshaft Woodruff key will be pointing toward the top side of the engine (arrow).

After the camshaft was installed and all the bearings were rechecked for proper seating, Bob lubricated the valve lifters with common wheel bearing grease. This will keep the lifters from falling out of the case half during the final engine assembly.

He then installed the valve lifters in the case half that contained our crankshaft assembly and the camshaft.

Again he squirted engine oil on all bearing surfaces to ensure proper lubrication.

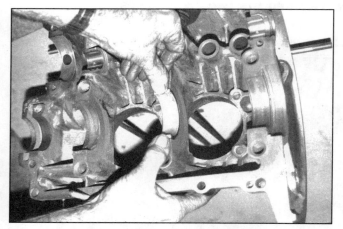

With everything assembled correctly in our main engine case half Bob then took our only remaining main bearing half and installed it into the other engine case half, making sure it seated properly on its alignment pin. At the same time, he installed the three remaining cam bearings in the case.

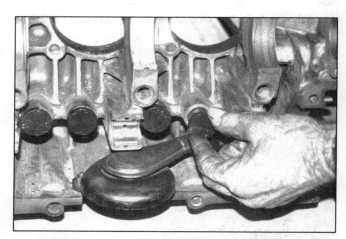

Bob then installed the remaining four greased valve lifters.

Now with everything checked and double checked and ready for the two case halves to be put together, Bob put a light coat of Permatex aviation sealer on the rear camshaft plug.

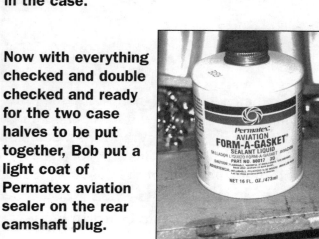

He then installed the camshaft plug in the engine case. CAUTION: Do not get any sealer on the camshaft or bearings.

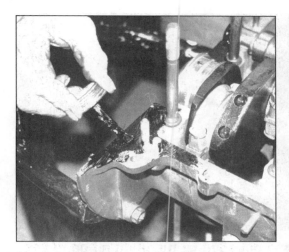

Next he lightly coated both case halves with sealer. Again, before assembling both case halves, double check to make sure everything is in place.

Bob now installed the two case halves.

He then lightly tapped them together.

Next he used a silicone sealer where the six large case nuts and washers install on the case.

He then installed the washers and nuts and torqued them to factory specs.

Bob tightened these nuts by using a staggered sequence.

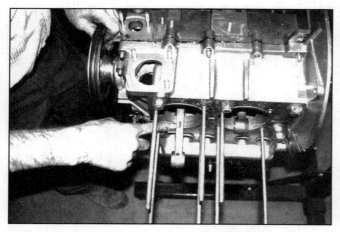

After torquing to specs, and with all forge marks on the connecting rods pointing up, the crankshaft turned over smoothly by hand, indicating that all was well at this point.

He then proceeded to the installation of the other case nuts with washers and torqued them to factory specs.

We opted to purchase a complete engine nut kit with locking nuts.

Using a pair of normal snap-ring pliers, Bob installed one wrist pin circlip in the first piston.

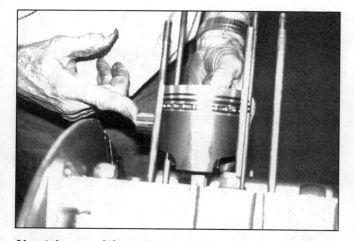

Next he positioned the piston on the rod, then slid the wrist pin through the rod until it stopped at the previously installed circlip.

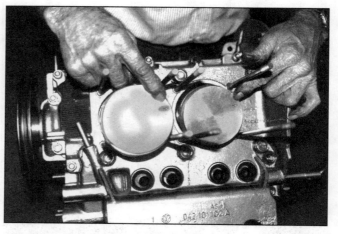

Bob made sure the arrows on the pistons pointed toward the flywheel end of the engine.

Illustrated here is the arrow that is stamped into the piston.

He then installed the second circlip on the wrist pin.

Bob next installed the piston ring compressor on the piston, making sure the rings were staggered so no notches lined up together.

After he had the ring compressor in place, he then oiled the piston rings with 10w40 engine oil.

He then installed the paper gasket on the end of the cylinder that seats to the engine block.

When installing the cylinder on the piston, Bob made sure that the flat side of the cylinder pointed inward (arrow).

Bob then moved to the next piston on the same side of the engine, repeating the same procedure. This photo shows both cylinders properly installed with the flat sides of the cylinders pointing inward.

With the cylinders properly in place, he then installed the air deflectors between the bottom of the cylinders at the center studs.

He then made sure that they clipped securely in place. CAUTION: This air deflector is an absolute must for proper cylinder cooling.

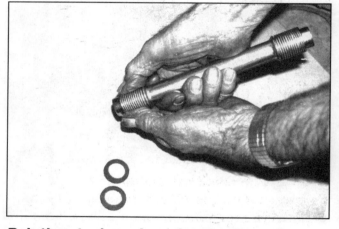

Bob then took each push-rod tube and grasped it as shown here and lightly stretched them by working the accordion end of the tube outward with his thumbs, to produce a proper seal with the cylinder head and case.

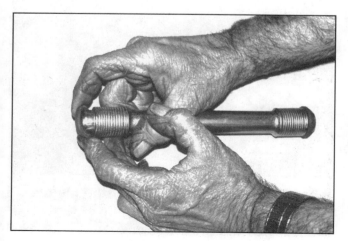

He then installed tube seals on both ends with the beveled edge toward the end of the tube. He did this on all eight tube seals.

Bob could now set the cylinder head on the guide studs and with four push rod tubes in place, he made sure that the seams on the tubes were in the up position, or pointing toward the piston and cylinder.

He then seated the cylinder head on the push-rod tubes and the pistons and cylinders.

Bob then installed all the washers and nuts on the cylinder head studs and torqued them to proper factory specifications using the proper torque sequence.

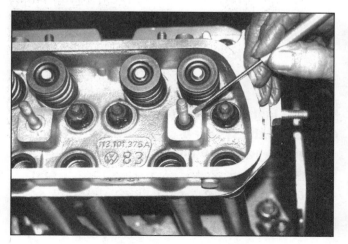

Bob then installed two rocker seals on the rocker studs of the cylinder head.

He then inserted the four push rods.

Next, the rocker arm assembly was installed as shown in these two shots.

Then came the wavy washers.

Next were the rocker retaining nuts.

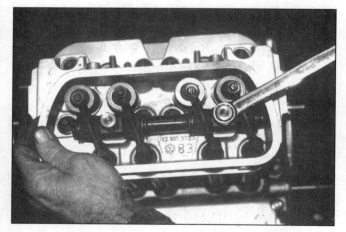

These nuts were then torqued to factory specifications. (The valves will all be adjusted later on in the engine rebuilding process.) Then Bob went to the other side of the engine and repeated the same procedure.

CAUTION: When moving an engine while it's on the engine stand, be aware that it can tip over and crash to the floor, causing irreparable damage to the cylinder head, as seen here (arrow). The only way to remedy this was to buy a new cylinder head, and commit the extra labor to install it.

For the oil pump installation the first thing Bob did was to install the paper gasket to the engine block, making sure he used the gasket with the proper hole size. Do not use any gasket sealer with this installation.

He installed the oil pump housing.

Then Bob lightly tapped the unit with a plastic-head hammer. If using a high-volume oil pump which has a thicker casting, it will be necessary to back the oil pump studs out approximately 1/4-inch.

Bob then installed the upper oil pump gear, making sure it seated properly in the camshaft slot. There are different types of camshafts that have slots with different depths; check with your camshaft supplier and match the camshaft to the oil pump.

The lower gear was the next item to be installed.

He next installed the outer oil pump gasket.

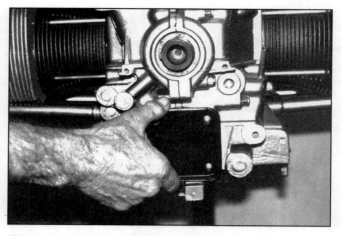

Then came the oil pump cover.

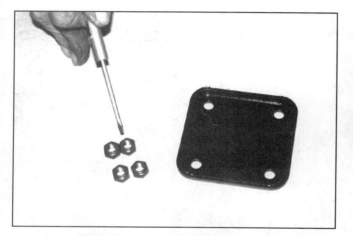

Bob then installed the four seal nuts.

He secured the four oil pump cover nuts.

Next he installed the first oil screen gasket.

Then the oil screen itself was dropped in place along with a second gasket.

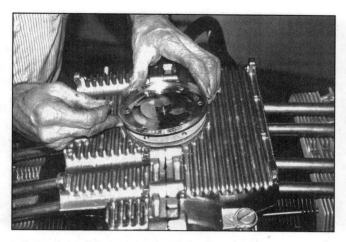

Then came the oil screen cover (left), with the copper gaskets and nuts (right), which were tightened down with a 10-mm wrench.

We now have what is referred to as an assembled long block.

Bob then installed the new crank pulley on the crankshaft.

He then tapped the crank pulley into place with a plastic-head hammer, installed the retaining nut and washer, and tightened the assembly.

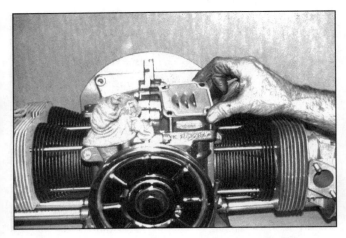

When installing the generator stand shim, the metal shim went on first with the vents in the position shown.

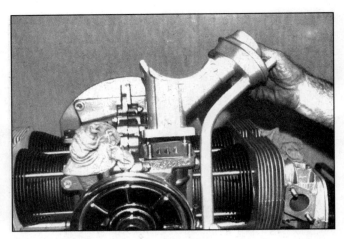

Then Bob installed the stand on the engine block.

He then secured the unit with four nuts and washers.

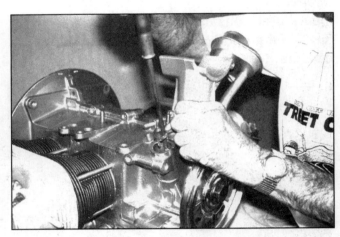

When installing the distributor drive gear washers, the first thing is to lower the two flat washers into the block. Do this by first inserting a long screwdriver, or similar device, down into the drive gear slot with the washers around this tool. Let the washers slide into place, making sure that they remain in position by first putting some grease on the washers.

Next comes the distributor drive. With the crank pulley on top dead center and number one cylinder on the compression stroke (both valves will be closed), carefully install the distributor drive gear. You can do this by inserting a common pencil into the upper hole as demonstrated here.

When the drive gear is installed, the offset slot should be at approximately a 4:00 position as indicated here, so that the distributor rotor points to the notch on the distributor housing. If the distributor is installed properly, this will be number one in the firing order.

The drive gear spring was installed using a pocket magnet or similar tool. Note: Make sure that the spring stays in the center of the drive gear.

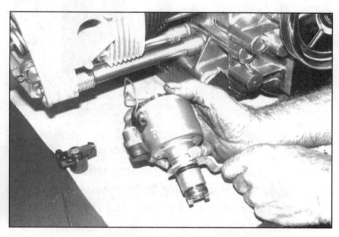

Then he installed the distributor and distributor clamp or hold down.

Next, he secured the hold down to the block. Final timing adjustments will be made after the engine has been started and warmed up.

To install the fuel pump, Bob first installed the lower fuel pump flange gasket.

Then the fuel pump flange.

Next he installed the fuel pump push rod.

Then came the upper flange gasket.

Bob then set the fuel pump on the mounting studs.

Finally, he installed the retaining nuts and bolted everything together.

It was now time to install four new oil cooler seals. Bob started by installing the two cooler seals that go between the two cooler sections.

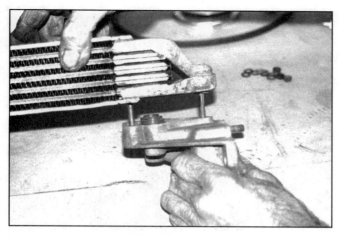

He then assembled the two pieces together.

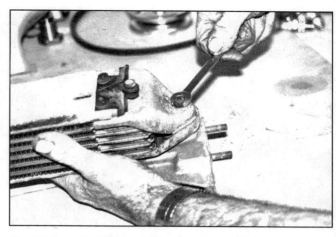

And then tightened them securely.

Bob then installed the two oil cooler seals that sit on the engine block. NOTE: Be sure to use the proper seals.

Next Bob installed the completed oil cooler assembly on the engine.

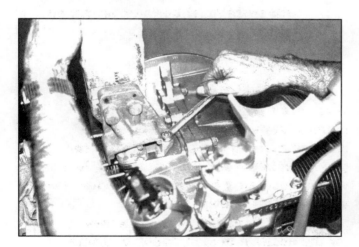

He then used the wavy washers and nuts to secure the unit to the engine.

For the flywheel installation, Bob started by replacing the rubber O-ring in the groove on the side of the flywheel that faces the crankshaft.

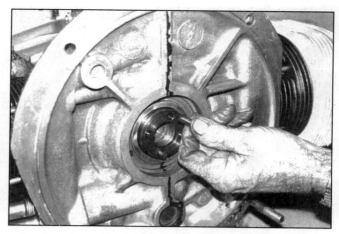

Next he installed the four dowel pins in the crankshaft. These pins will occasionally pop back out, so make sure they seat properly before proceeding.

Bob then installed the three crank shims on the crankshaft. Do not install the crank seal until after the end play has been checked.

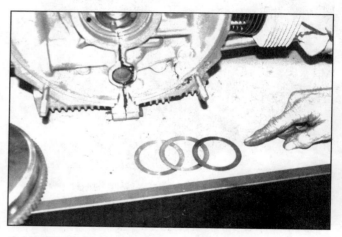

CAUTION: There must be three shims, no more, no less.

If you are using the same shims that came with the engine you are rebuilding, there is a possibility the end play adjustment will be okay. If not, it will be necessary to adjust for proper end play. This is done by using a micrometer to gauge shim thickness for the addition or subtraction of shims for proper end play, along with a dial indicator for determining crankshaft thrust bearing end play. This application called for .008.

Bob then inserted the new crank seal in position.

He then carefully tapped it in place using a plastic-head hammer.

After the end play had been set, Bob installed the flywheel.

He then secured it with a new gland nut, and torqued it to the proper spec. Proper torquing of this nut is critical.

Bob used an air impact gun to start the tightening.

Now we moved ahead to the clutch installation. First, Bob lubricated the pilot bearing in the flywheel gland nut.

He then installed the clutch disc on a pilot shaft.

Next he inserted the pilot shaft into the pilot bearing.

Then he installed the clutch cover (pressure plate) and secured it with bolts and washers.

After torquing these to specifications, he removed the pilot shaft.

Before installing the engine on the transmission, Bob made sure the clutch release bearing and clips are properly installed.

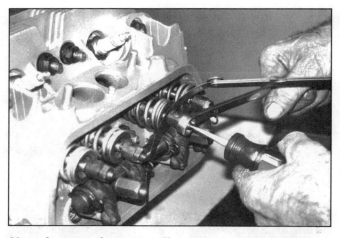

Now it was time to adjust the valves. With the engine at top dead center on number one cylinder, Bob adjusted the valves to specifications, which were .006 on this stock 1600 VW Bug engine.

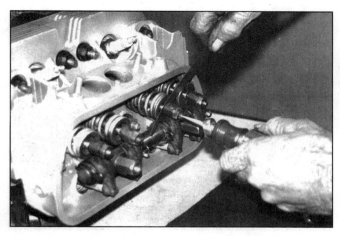

He made sure it was a snug fit with the feeler gauge, but not too tight.

He then cranked the engine clockwise to number two cylinder and adjusted the valves as on number one cylinder. Then he cranked the engine to number three cylinder and adjusted the valves, finally cranking the engine to number four cylinder and adjusting its valves accordingly. With this accomplished, the valves should be ready to go.

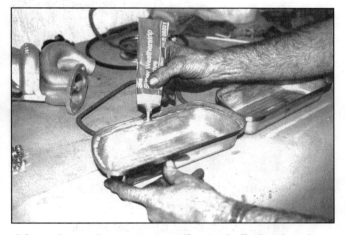

After the valves were adjusted, Bob glued the valve cover gaskets to the valve covers. Do not glue the gaskets to the cylinder heads.

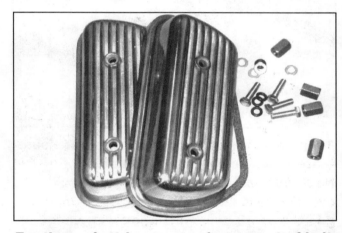

For the project buggy we chose a set of bolt on valve covers.

Bob then mounted the valve covers on the cylinder heads, and secured them with retaining bolts.

Installing the oil sending unit is not a particularly difficult task. Bob begins by gently starting the oil sending unit into the block by hand.

He then used a wrench to tighten it snugly, but was very careful not to over tighten.

Next, Bob installed the spark plugs and cylinder head tins. First, he had to properly gap the spark plugs, using a feeler gauge or gaping tool.

Bob started each plug by hand in its respective hole, then torqued them to spec. Do not over tighten as thread damage can occur.

Next he installed the cylinder head tins.

Bob then secured everything with proper screws and washers. Note the clean, dry shop rag inserted into the intake part of the cylinder head to avoid any foreign objects accidentally falling into the cylinder.

Next on the agenda is the intake manifold assembly. The intake manifold consists of five basic pieces, plus four clamps. They are: right and left intake manifolds.

One center manifold mounts to the engine block and holds the carburetor, plus two intake rubber boots which are held in place by the four clamps.

After lubricating the rubber boots and installing them on the center manifold, Bob installed the four clamps on the boots. (He did not tighten those clamps at this time.)

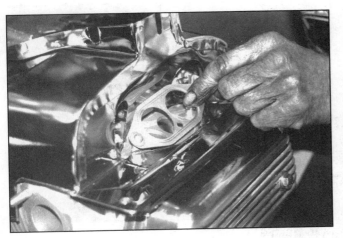

After removing the shop rag from the intake ports and before putting the assembly on the engine, Bob installed new gaskets on each cylinder head intake port.

To install the intake manifold assembly required some slight maneuvering, but because Bob had left the intake boot clamps loose, until the unit had been completely installed, the installation went together without a hitch.

He then tightened the nuts at both cylinder head intake ports.

Bob then secured the center intake support nut.

To finish the intake manifold installation, Bob tightened the four clamps on the intake boots.

The engine is starting to take shape.

After the generator brushes had been inspected and/or replaced, Bob carefully set the finished generator/fan shroud over the oil cooler and onto the engine.

He then secured the unit with new shroud screws and then installed the generator strap with bolt and nut.

Bob then made sure the Woodruff key was in the slot on the generator output shaft.

Next he installed the inner generator pulley section.

Next were the belt adjustment shims. NOTE: It will be necessary to add or subtract the number of adjustment shims in order to come up with the proper fan belt tension.

Finally, Bob installed the outer generator pulley section and the fan belt, tightening the retaining nut accordingly.

Exhaust systems come in all shapes and sizes. I chose a chrome unit with a quieter muffler. This photo shows the completed exhaust system.

The first step was to install the exhaust gaskets on the cylinder head exhaust ports.

To install this exhaust system, the shorter tubes go to the rear of the engine (arrow).

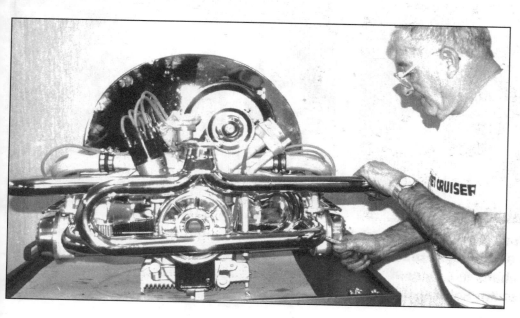

The longer tubes with the four tube connectors go in the front, with the muffler attaching to the four pipes that come together at the front of the engine.

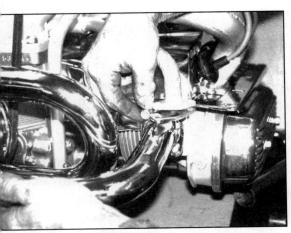

After the exhaust system had been set in place, Bob installed and secured all exhaust manifold nuts. Installing any exhaust system is like working a puzzle, but with patience and persistence, it will come together.

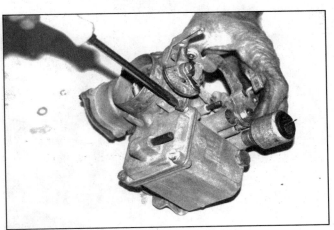

Rebuilding and installing a one-barrel VW carb is a very basic procedure, about as simple as the carb itself. Start by removing the five upper retaining screws (left) and lifting off the bowl cover (right).

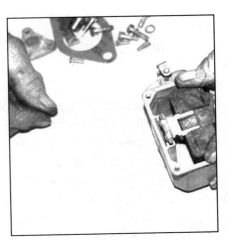
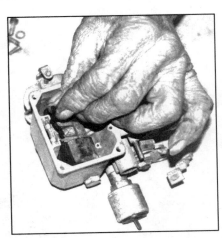
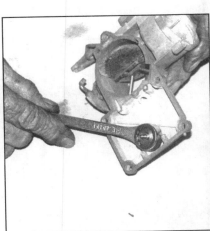

Remove the float (left) and retaining clip (right) from the bowl. At this time check to insure that there is no fuel inside the float. You can do this by gently shaking the float and listening for a sloshing sound.

Remove the needle and seat assembly from the bowl cover.

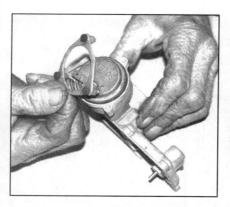 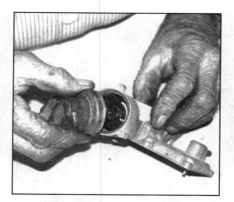 

Remove the choke assembly as shown in the three photos above.

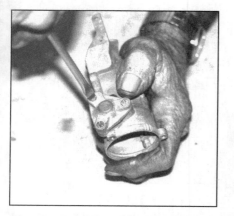 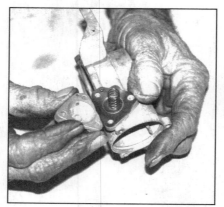 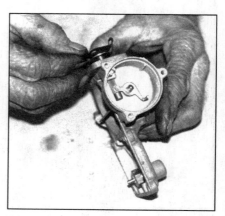

Next, remove the choke unloader diaphragm from the upper bowl cover as shown in this sequence of photos.

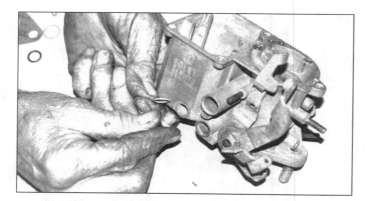

Remove the bowl drain plug.

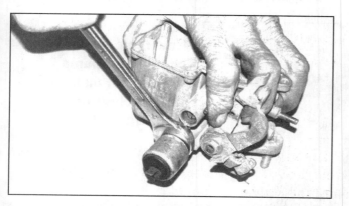 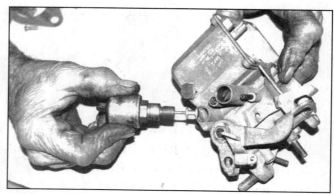

The fuel cutoff solenoid is then removed as shown in these two photos.

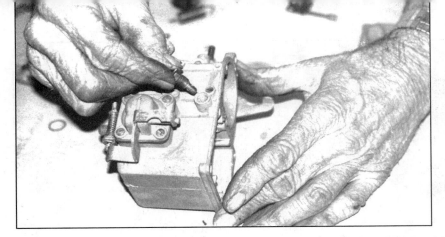

The low idle jet comes out with a quick twist of a screwdriver.

Now the high-speed upper jet is extracted with surgical precision.

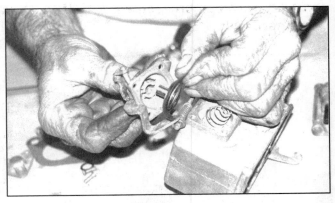

The main jet is then removed with equal precision.

Now remove the accelerator pump diaphragm, plus the accelerator discharge tube.

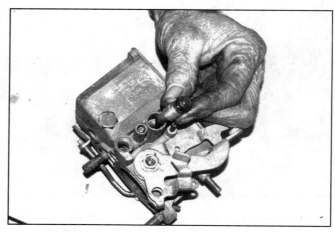

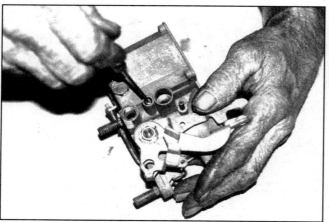

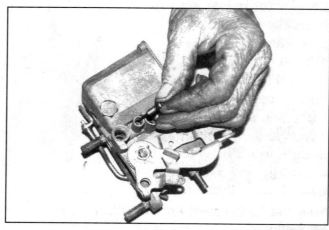

Finally, remove the air-fuel screws. After a thorough cleaning in carb cleaner, air dry or blow parts dry with compressed air. CAUTION: Always wear safety goggles when using compressed air.

After a thorough cleaning, the carburetor is primed for reassembly.

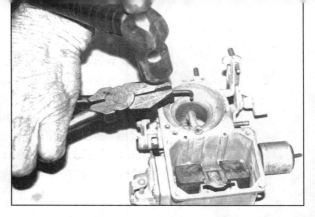

Install the accelerator pump discharge tube and upper gasket. At this point, the carb bowl is ready. Install the choke unloader diaphragm, choke inner cover and choke coil with retaining ring and screws. Set bowl cover in place and install five screws and secure.

Carburetor reassembly is basically a reverse procedure of the disassembly process. We started by installing the carb accelerator pump with the pump spring first and then the pump diaphragm. Secure it with the four retaining screws. Do not over tighten these four screws. Install the low idle jet and secure it (just snug). Install the high speed upper jet and install the main jet in the bottom of the carb and secure them. Now mount the bowl drain plug with a new gasket. Next, install 1 - Air/fuel mixture screw; 2 - Idle screw; 3 - Fuel shut off solenoid. Then install the float and hold down clip.

Install idle screw and accelerator return spring.

When mounting the carb on the intake manifold, use the proper base gasket. Note: It is easier to install the carburetor if the distributor cap is off.

Then secure the carb to the intake with locking nuts. Make sure all linkage works free and easy. Then hook up the accelerator cable and electric choke wire.

After making sure there was no wear in the clutch shaft and bushing, Bob installed the clutch release bearing, and the retaining clips, with the smooth disc surface facing out. We were now ready to install the engine and hook it up to the transmission. NOTE: Lightly lube the transmission output shaft for easier installation of the engine.

While the engine was still on the workbench, Bob installed the distributor cap and wires. Before installing the engine there are some things to check and double-check. First, make sure you have new oil in the engine. Then check to make sure all the clutch pressure plate bolts are tight, the clutch release bearing has been installed properly, the pilot bearing in the flywheel gland nut has been lubricated, the starter bushings inspected and replaced if needed, and that all the transmission bolts are secured.

After the preinstallation checklist had been covered, item by item, Bob was ready to set the completed engine on a floor jack.

Bob then positioned the engine so that the hole in the clutch pressure plate lined up with the transmission main shaft. Also, the lower engine alignment studs were aligned with their respective transmission holes.

With this done, Bob proceeded to gently guide the engine into place.

He then secured the powerplant with mounting bolts and nuts.

With the engine installed and bolted in place, our project engine assembly was looking great.

Wiring Your Dune Buggy

It's Easier Than You Think!

Wiring a dune buggy is not nearly as complicated as you might imagine. On the following pages you will find a front wiring schematic, a rear wiring schematic and a dash console or center wiring schematic, all of which have been laid out as simply as possible to avoid confusing anyone. These are basic wiring schematics that will include headlights, high and low beam, a high beam indicator light; turn signals, right and left; stop lights; parking lights, and the basic charging system and starting system.

First, if you intend to drive your dune buggy on public highways, check with your local vehicle inspection station so you can comply with your state's codes and regulations.

After installing all lights, the gauge and switch panel, gauges and switches, horn, voltage regulator and the complete engine, we were now ready to start our wiring project. Other than a few miscellaneous cosmetic items, the wiring system was about the last thing done to the dune

CAUTION:
The schematics and wiring procedures described in this chapter may be illegal for highway use in your area; check state and local regulations before proceeding.

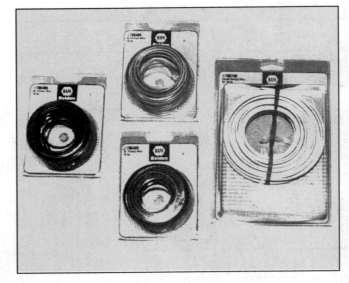

With the gauges, lights and other electrical equipment installed, we were ready to wire the dune buggy. First, we needed individual rolls of colored wire.

When we mounted our fuse panel inside the storage box, we used individual wires from the fuse panel to the fused circuits.

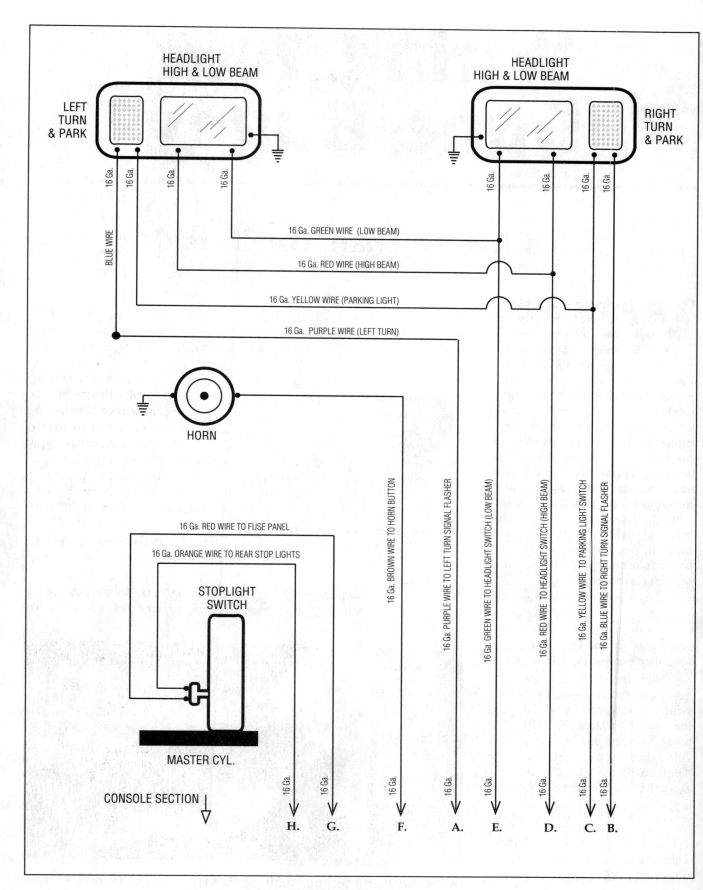

FRONT WIRING DIAGRAM: Figure 1.1

FRONT WIRING SECTION: Figure 1.1

DO THIS SECTION FIRST

Actual wiring lengths needed to wire a dune buggy will vary for a number of reasons, including buggy frame length, location of lights and accessories, location of the fuse panel, and direction of wire routing. Approximate lengths of wire from each light or switch on the average dune buggy are 10 feet. There were eight single wires in this section.

After using wire connectors to connect all wires to lights and switches, or soldering them, wrap the other end with a piece of masking tape and label each one for its appropriate switch or light, such as left front turn signal, headlight low beam, etc.

The gauges or sizes of the different wiring used were:

- 16 gauge — horn, lights, electric instruments, etc.
- 12 gauge — ignition switch power supply, generator and voltage regulator.
- 4 gauge — battery cables, both positive and negative.

NOTE: Always allow extra length for final assembly at the console section.

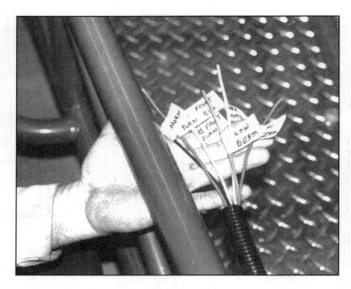

As you run your wiring, tag the end of each wire, identifying the position of each wire in the wiring schematic, such as right rear turn signal, left front turn signal, etc.

buggy. We chose to purchase all of the wire that was needed for the wiring project in individual rolls of color-coded wire.

We started the wiring by measuring from the left rear brake, park and turn signal unit, along the back of the buggy, and down the right inside of the buggy frame, to the front frame bar, then up and across to the gauge and switch panel, allowing at least 12 inches of excess wire for each switch or gauge.

When we measured for the wiring that was needed for the front of the buggy, we started at the left front headlight and turn signal unit, then across the front of the buggy and again down the right inside of

the buggy frame rail to the front frame bar, then up and across to the gauge and switch panel, again allowing 12 inches of excess on each individual wire. When we mounted our fuse panel inside the storage box, we used individual wires from the fuse panel to the fused circuits. TECH TIP: An optional way to fuse your accessories is to use in-line fuse holders which I have used many times in the past with excellent results. These are available at most auto parts stores.

NOTE: As you progress through the wiring procedure it will be necessary to tag the end of each wire, identifying each wire's position in the wiring schematic, such as left

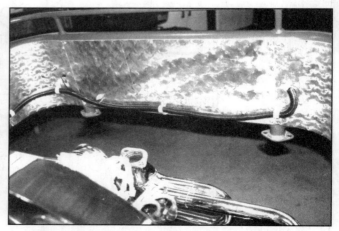

After carefully identifying and tagging each wire, we installed the wires collectively through wire loom and then routed the loom along the right inside of the dune buggy frame rail (left) and at the rear of the buggy (right).

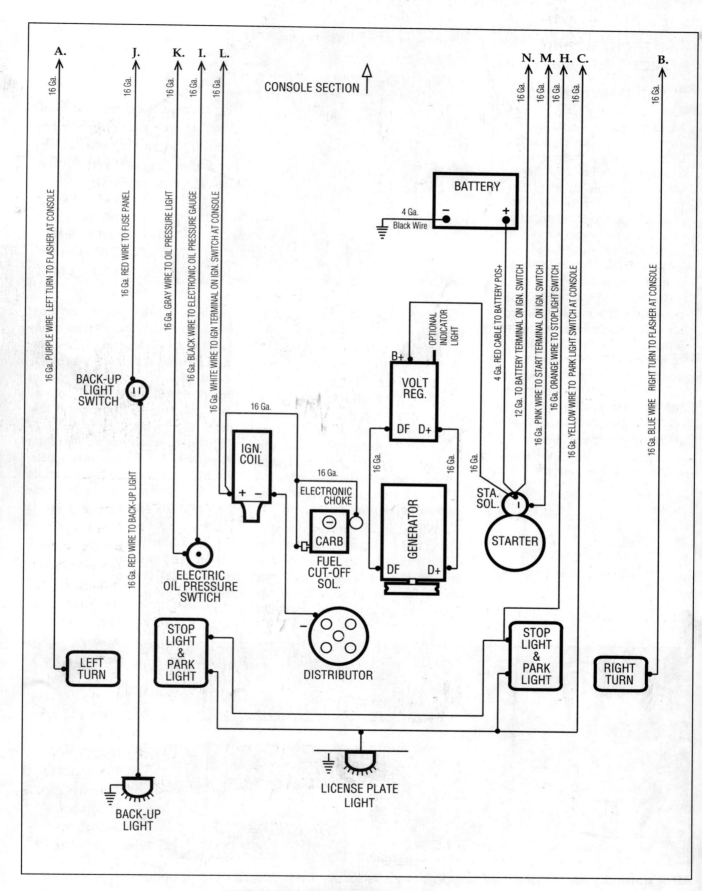

REAR WIRING DIAGRAM: Figure 1.2

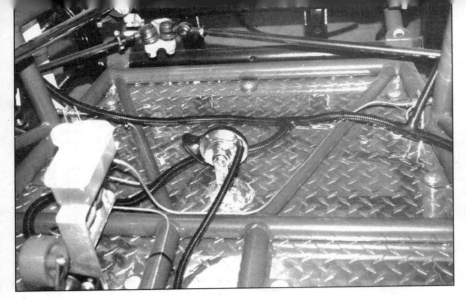

The loom will be secured with tie straps or loom connectors both in the front (left), along the sides (below, left), and in the rear (below, right).

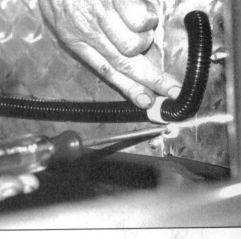

REAR WIRING SECTION: Figure 1.2

DO THIS SECTION SECOND

Rear wiring will proceed as in the front section. However, certain components, such as the voltage regulator, generator, and starter, will require wiring of a heavier gauge (12 gauge), so this wiring will be cut to length and positioned to avoid interference with any moving engine parts or hot exhaust.

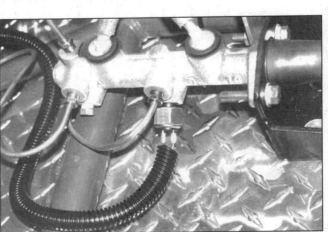

rear turn signal, right front turn signal, etc.

After carefully identifying and tagging each wire, we installed the wires collectively through wire loom and then routed the loom along the right inside of the dune buggy frame rail. The loom was secured with tie straps or loom connectors both in the front and in the rear. Using wire loom and proper wire connectors makes for a workable and neat wiring harness.

TECH TIP: Keep all wiring and wire loom on the inside of the frame rail and properly secured. By color coding all the wiring rather than using all one-color wire, the final hook up at the dash console will go much easier. A color-coded schematic will also simplify and expedite the diagnosis of any future wiring problems.

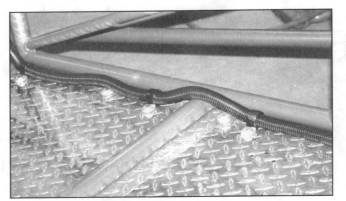

Using wire loom and proper wire loom holders makes for a workable and neat wiring harness as depicted in these photos showing the front of the buggy near the master cylinder (left, top), and along the right side of the frame (left, bottom).

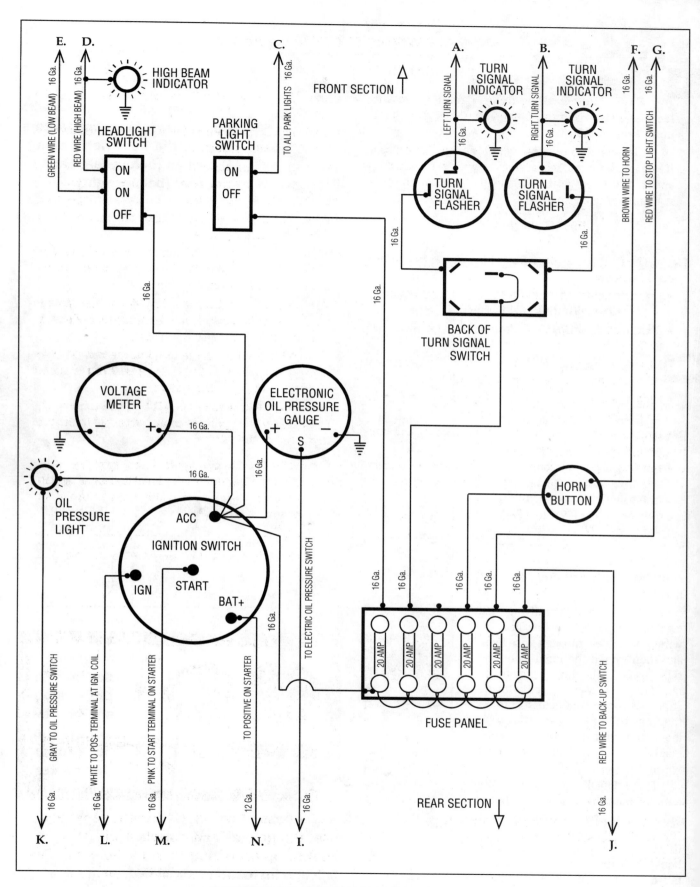

CONSOLE WIRING DIAGRAM: Figure 1.3

CONSOLE WIRING SECTION: Figure 1.3

DO THIS SECTION LAST

NOTE: Run all wiring from 1.1 and 1.2 in wire loom and secure to the frame rail before final hook-up in section 1.3.

It is now time to wire everything into the console. If you properly marked all the wires from section 1.1 and 1.2, use the wiring schematic, 1.3, for the final hook-up at the console.

FINAL WIRING HOOK-UP AT THE CONSOLE: SECTION 1.3

The final wiring hook-up at the console should proceed as follows:

- Left turn signal wires (A) front and rear will connect to (A) at the left turn signal flasher.
- Right turn signal wires (B) front and rear will connect to (B) at the right turn signal flasher.
- Parking light wire (C) from the front and rear will connect at (C) on the parking light switch.
- High beam wire (D) from the front section will connect at (D) on the headlight switch.
- Low beam wire (E) from the front section will connect at (E) on the headlight switch.
- Horn wire (F) will connect to horn button (F) at console, then run the remaining horn button wire to the fuse panel.
- Brake light wire (G) will connect to the fuse panel.

- Brake light wire (H) will connect to the rear brake lights.
- Electronic oil pressure gauge wire (I) will connect at the oil pressure switch.
- Wire (J) will connect to one side of the back-up light switch on the transmission. The other wire from the back-up light switch will go to the back-up light itself.
- Wire (K) will connect the oil pressure light to the oil pressure switch on the engine.
- Wire (L), which is the ignition run wire, will connect from the ignition side of the ignition switch to the positive terminal on the ignition coil.
- Wire (M) will run from the start side of the ignition switch to the starter solenoid terminal that will energize the starter to crank the engine.
- Wire (N) will run from the terminal marked BAT+ on the ignition switch to the positive post of the starter solenoid to energize the system.
- The battery will require one (1) negative cable to the frame and one (1) positive cable connected to the positive post on the starter.

CAUTION: Always wear safety goggles when working near a battery; never smoke near a battery; and never wear jewelry, especially rings, when working on or near a battery.

With these wires routed and connected as shown, along with the wires from the fuse panel to the switches, this system worked very well on the project dune buggy.

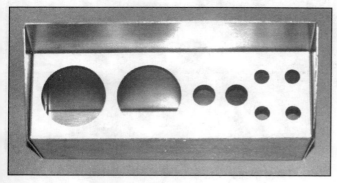

Here's a typical console or switch panel, pre-cut, pre-formed and ready for installation.

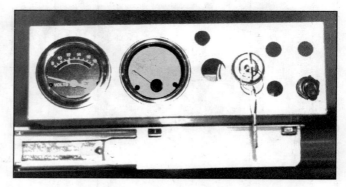

Regardless of which instrument panel you use, the gauges and switches will be hooked up according to the schematic. The finished installation should resemble this.

To mount the ignition coil and voltage regulator, a flat and sturdy surface is necessary. I accomplished this by taking an 8x8x1/8-inch piece of soft aluminum and bending a 1-inch lip on two sides and then drilling two holes in each lip.

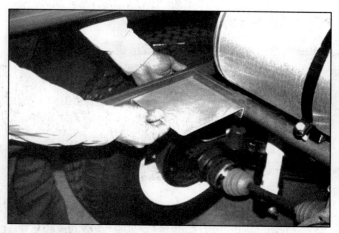

Then we positioned the plate on the left rear corner of the frame rail (above, left) and drilled four mounting holes through the plate into the frame rail (above, right), bolting it in place. The result was this very sanitary looking installation (below, left).

Locate the ignition coil and voltage regulator in the desired position, remembering to allow clearance for wire connectors and wires.

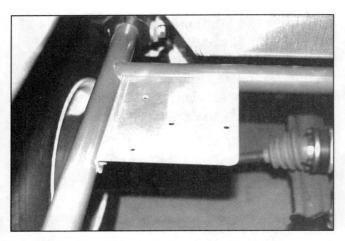

Mark the mounting holes with a magic marker, drill them, and then bolt the coil and regulator in place.

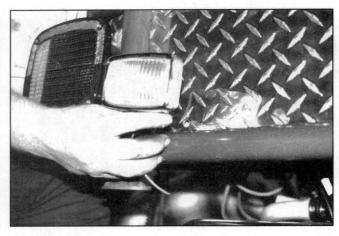

Add-on lights, such as this auxiliary back-up light, are easy to install.

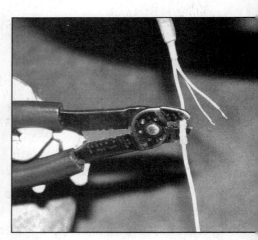

We used a crimping tool and wire connectors to connect all wires to the lights and switches.

To mount the back-up lights, you simply drill holes to mount either one or two light units, run one single wire to connect the two lights, route that wire to one side of the back-up light switch on the transmission, and then run one wire from the fuse panel to the other side of the back-up light switch. The completed installation will look like this.

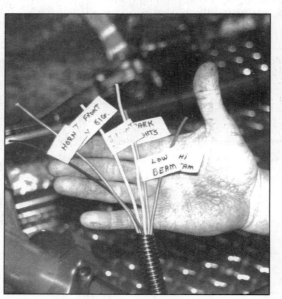

Then we wrapped the other ends with masking tape and labeled them for the appropriate switch or light, such as left rear turn signal, headlight low beam, horn, etc. After following the schematic and installing the wiring harness, it is time to wire everything at the dash panel.

Shown here is the panel after it has been fully wired.

If you properly marked all the wires and accurately followed the wiring schematic, the rear of the dash panel should look like this, or something similar to this with other dash designs.

There are many commercially available dash consoles one can use for his dune buggy, or with the right equipment one can construct his own custom dash panel. No matter what style of dash panel you end up with, the gauges and switches will hook up as the accompanying schematics show.

A typical factory-made wiring harness will average about $50 and up depending on the options on the dune buggy. To make my own wiring harness from rolls of wire, it priced out to less than $30. It has been my own personal experience that it is easier to wire a dune buggy from scratch using this wiring schematic with readily available wire than try-ing to decipher and route a pre-made wiring harness. Past experience has also taught me to mount items such as the ignition coil and voltage regulator away from the engine and not on the engine shroud. Engine vibration is a fact of life and is the main reason these protective measures must be taken.

To mount the ignition coil and voltage regulator requires a flat and sturdy surface. I provided this by taking an 8x8x1/8-inch piece of soft aluminum and bending 1-inch lips on two sides and then drilling two holes in each lip and securing the plate in the left rear corner of the dune buggy.

I then located the ignition coil and voltage regulator on the plate, remembering to allow adequate clearance for wire connectors and wires. I then marked the mounting holes with a magic marker, drilled the holes with a power drill, and bolt-ed the coil and regulator in place.

Add-on lights, such as auxiliary back-up lights, are simple to install. Just drill holes to mount either one or two light units, run one single wire to connect the two lights, route that wire to one side of the back-up light switch on the transmission, and then run one wire from the fuse panel to the other side of the back-up light switch. ∎

NOTES

_____

_____

_____

_____

_____

Non-Skid Tape

Protecting the Tree Bars

The tree bars — the rails that extend out and run alongside the buggy — serve more than one purpose. First, they protect the rear wheels from being struck by trees or other objects. Second, they can be used as running boards to make it easier to enter and exit the dune buggy.

However, after using them as a step to get in and out of the dune buggy on several occasions, I noticed that the paint was being scratched all the way down to the metal. Also, when it's wet or muddy, they become very slippery and are almost dangerous to step on. So, to eliminate these problems, I purchased a roll of non-skid tape, which was easily applied to the tree bars. This served two purposes in protecting the paint from damage and providing a non-skid surface for entering and exiting the dune buggy. ∎

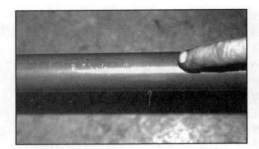

Using the tree bars to enter and exit the buggy is a natural exercise, but it scars the bars, chipping and scratching through the paint and primer right down to the metal.

A quality non-skid tape rated for outdoor use was selected. It's commonly available at automotive and hardware stores.

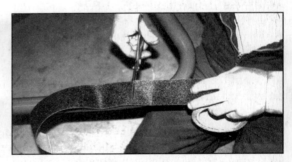

Cut the tape to fit your bars. This roll was two inches wide by five yards long, which was plenty to handle our installation on both tree bars.

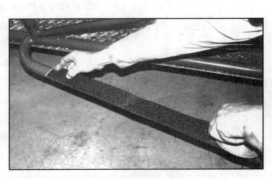

The tape is adhesive backed and all you need to do is peel the paper backing off and apply the tape.

With the new tape in position, getting in and out of the buggy became a lot easier and safer. The non-skid surface is very effective.

Fabricating the Body Panels

Custom Coachbuilding

Many dune buggies are built and operated without a body, but the rig is much more comfortable, much more pleasant to drive on the open road and definitely safer with full body armor. To protect yourself and your passenger or passengers from airborne debris, bugs, rain and wind, only a complete body structure can fill the bill. And, there's a wide and wild variety of neat body configurations possible, virtually anything the mind can imagine.

The most popular frames available have fiberglass bodies available for them, many of which can merely be bolted in place. These come in many shapes, sizes and colors to match one's personal tastes.

After deciding to have a local shop build the body for our dune buggy, we took the rolling, running project to Waco Enterprises, Sidney, Ohio, where owner Wayne Watercutter greeted us and welcomed our buggy into his well equipped shop.

Watercutter examines the dune buggy, evaluating it for different body concepts. Wayne builds and drives oval track race cars so he was the perfect choice to design and manufacture the body panels for the buggy. He then tied colored string at different points on the frame to have straight lines from which to measure and work.

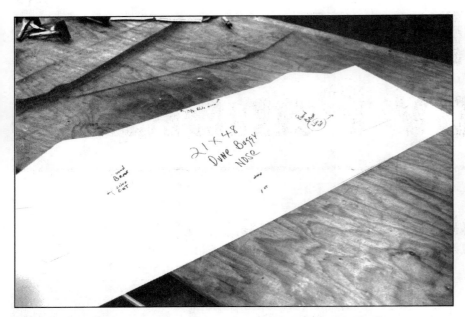

Wayne custom designs each piece of the body to fit perfectly and then removes that panel, which is then marked and kept for a pattern for the manufacturing of additional panels.

He used a sheet of aluminum with a thickness of .040 and these sheets come painted and with a plastic covering for protection during shipping and cutting or forming operations. The plastic covering must be removed before installation.

Or, one can build his own body. It's tedious, difficult and can be expensive, but it's not impossible. Another option is to have a professional fabricate a body for you. We decided to follow the latter route.

We were fortunate to have someone available locally who could handle a body-building project for us. So I made an appointment with Wayne Watercutter, Waco Racing Enterprises, Sidney, Ohio, and took the body-less project buggy to his shop. He had a space reserved for my buggy. Wayne builds and races oval track race cars so he was the perfect choice to design and took the body panels for the buggy.

The first thing he did was to look it over in general and get some ideas on where to start. He then began the process by tying colored string at different points on the frame to have straight lines from which to measure and work. His many years of experience in repairing race car bodies guided him through the rather complicated and time-consuming process of measuring, cutting, bending, and hand forming the first versions of the body panels.

Wayne first custom designs each piece of the body to fit perfectly and then removes that panel, which is marked and kept as a pattern for manufacturing additional panels. He used the same type of sheet aluminum that he uses on his oval track cars. Its thickness is .040 and it has a very glossy baked-on paint finish, which has proven quite durable. These sheets of aluminum come with a plastic covering for protection during shipping, as well as handling, cutting, forming, etc.

He first designed a workable two-piece front nose section that eliminated the tunnel effect, whereby rocks, wind, rain, etc., are funneled back into the driver's compartment. We also bought and installed a tow-bar bracket for the ease of hooking up to a tow vehicle. It's a universal tow-bar bracket that can be adapted to fit many different applications. All that was required to install it on the Pack Rat frame was to drill four

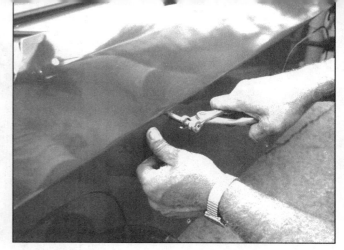

After both right and left rear side panels were made to fit perfectly, 3/16-inch holes were drilled.

The side panels were then installed using what is called a Cleko-Loc, a device that holds any body panel temporarily in place while the installer makes measurements for the rear side panels.

Both front and rear side panels were now completed.

3/8-inch holes in the bracket and use the proper length bolts with nuts and lock washers to secure it to the front nose of the buggy frame.

The Pack Rat frame comes with a flat bar welded on the nose section with four pre-drilled holes in it. The bolts, nuts and lock washers that you use for securing the bracket to the buggy frame must be industrial strength. CAUTION: Check with your parts supplier to see if these universal tow-bar brackets will safely adapt to your specific frame.

With the front nose section out of the way, he proceeded to design a hood for the buggy. We first thought we would need extra braces added to the buggy frame for hood support,

It was now time to tackle the front nose section. This turned out to be a real challenge. The main problem was the upward angles of the front bar assembly. Without fully enclosing the front section, a tunnel effect would have been created, letting wind, rocks, dirt and mud flow back into the driver's lap.

After some serious thought, a number of variations and design changes were developed. Finally, Watercutter came up with this workable two-piece front nose section. Note the tow-bar bracket that we installed for the ease of hooking up to a tow vehicle.

Watercutter then turned his attention to the hood. Here, he's forming the rear section of the hood in a metal break.

After using the metal break, he then finished the rear section via hand-forming.

but after just one design of the hood, it proved to be a very sturdy unit requiring no extra bracing. This was accomplished by rolling the outer edges over in a neat, smooth radius that created the extra strength needed. Wayne did this by devising a one-inch round bar fixture which he added to his metal break equipment for creating the smooth radius.

Also, he formed a smooth upward curve at the back of the hood which comes in contact with the lower frame bar of the window frame. After all the work required to design and build the panels was finished, Wayne decided to add an

A prototype hood is installed on the buggy to check for proper size, fit and clearance.

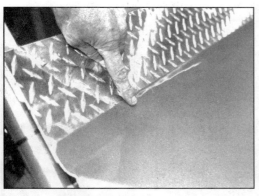

To fabricate the final version of the hood, Wayne incorporated the use of a round metal bar with the metal break to arrive at the smooth curved radius depicted here.

Wayne checks the final version of the hood and nose section for proper fit prior to installation.

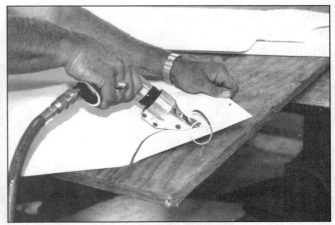

The aluminum panels are relatively easy to cut either by hand (left) or by using a power metal shear (right).

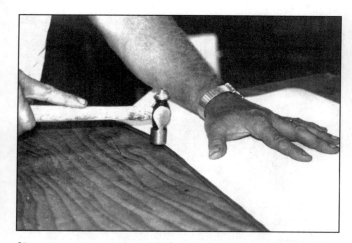

It was necessary at times to form rounded edges by gently tapping the panels' edges with a metal-head hammer.

After all the work required to design and build the side panels was finished, Wayne decided to add an inlaid effect on the panels.

inlaid effect to the side panels using a device called a bead roller. The effect was sensational.

When permanently installing the front nose section and side panels, several methods can be used. We used 3/16-inch pop rivets. Another method involves zip screws. These unique screws have their own drill-bit tips for drilling holes and securing the body panels as they are screwed into the framework. They do, however, require high-speed drills.

Locating someone with the talents of Wayne Watercutter, who can skillfully fabricate body panels to custom fit any buggy builder's project, was indeed fortunate. Yet there are shops of this type in nearly all medium to large cities, and even in small rural towns, so hopefully there's one near you. If not, you might attempt the building of your own body with professional guidance and assistance, or you can always order a frame for which factory designed and manufactured bodies are available.

With all the new panels installed on our project buggy, it took on a whole new personality. It even seemed to run better! ∎

With a device called a bead roller, the inlaid pattern was created. This added touch was perfect. It gave the normally flat panels some real pizzazz.

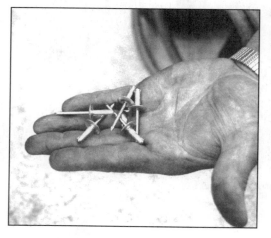

Now it was time to permanently install the panels, starting with the front nose section. In the previously drilled 3/16-inch holes, a panel-holding device called a pop rivet was used. These were also 3/16-inch. After the rivets were popped into place, the panels were permanently secured.

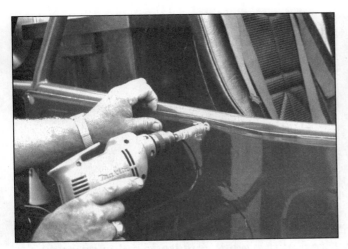

If it becomes necessary to remove pop rivets, they must be drilled out, as demonstrated here.

After the nose section was permanently in place, the rear side panels were installed using the same type of pop rivets. Then came the front side panels, again securing them with pop rivets.

Finally the hood was installed. It was adjusted to fit perfectly.

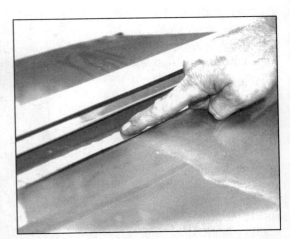

The hood fit into the designed-in lip on the front nose section, which was there to hold the hood in place.

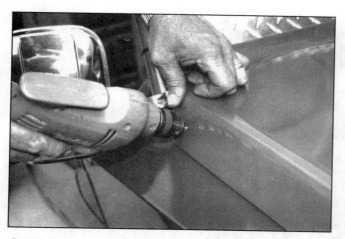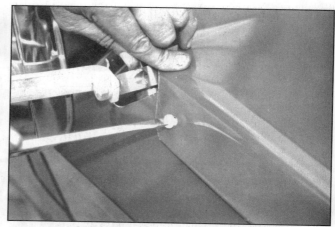

On the rear section of the hood, he drilled holes through the hood and the side panels (left) and secured the rear of the hood with two plastic screws and nuts (right). The reason for using plastic screws and nuts was primarily to prevent rusting. To remove the hood just use a screwdriver and remove the plastic screws, then lift the hood off, sliding it toward the rear and upward for easy access of the front section of the buggy.

Watercutter's talents for fabricating body panels made a nice finishing touch to our dune buggy project. The buggy is shown here with all of its panels installed.

Aligning the Front End

Getting on Track

Nothing will have you going in circles more than a front end that is badly out of alignment. My first run down the road confirmed that ... and quickly!

Prior to taking the dune buggy on its first road test, I had adjusted the tie rods and the upper ball joint camber as close as possible by just visually inspecting the front tires for alignment. They appeared to be rather straight, but after tightening all the tie rod and upper camber locking nuts and road testing the buggy, I discovered otherwise. The buggy did not handle properly on the highway, pulling both right and left and wandering from side to side, while requiring constant correction of the steering wheel just to keep it straight on the road. It was actually "unsafe at any speed." I then made an appointment with McLain's Service Center, Sidney, Ohio, to align the front suspension on our project buggy.

Upon arrival at the shop, Bob Varno, the alignment technician, had me pull the buggy on the alignment rack. He then proceeded to install what he called an "alignment head" on each wheel. These devices accurately measure caster, camber, toe-in, and four-wheel alignment by relaying the alignment specs of each individual wheel to the computer and comparing them to the preset measurements for a specific vehicle's suspen-

McLain's Service Center, Sidney, Ohio, would align the front suspension on our project buggy. After pulling the buggy onto the shop's alignment rack, Bob Varno, alignment technician, proceeded to install an "alignment head" on each wheel. These devices accurately measure caster, camber, and four-wheel alignment.

sion. The computer then displays on a screen where the suspension is now set and where it should be set to be aligned correctly.

It is also imperative that you make sure the wheelbase is the same on the right and left sides of the buggy before any wheel alignment is attempted. If there is a difference of 1/8 inch or more, this vehicle, or any other vehicle, will do what is referred to as dog tracking, where all four wheels are not tracking in the same straight and forward pattern. To check the wheelbase, measure from the center of a rear wheel to the center of a front wheel on the same side, then repeat the procedure on the other side. Both measurements must be the same.

Next, we removed the front hood to access the tie rods for adjustment. Bob asked what year and type of VW suspension was used on the dune buggy, and I informed him that it was a 1973 VW bug front suspen-

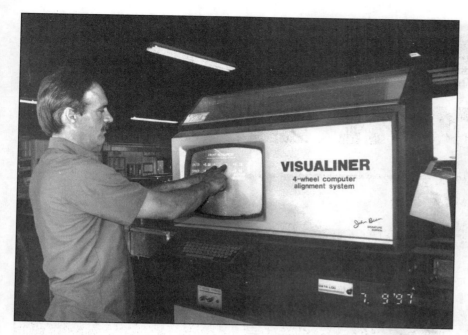

The readings are then relayed to the computer and compared with the preset measurements for a particular suspension. The computer then displays on a screen where the suspension is set and where it should be set to be aligned correctly. Make sure the wheelbase is the same on both sides of the buggy before wheel alignment is attempted.

sion. He proceeded to put this information into his alignment computer, which instantly displayed specifications and the preferred settings for that particular year Bug.

The preferred settings were: Caster + 2.00 positive for both left and right front wheels, camber + 0.52 positive for both left and right front wheels, and a toe-in of + 1/16-inch positive. There are allowable tolerances with a minimum of + 1.24 and a maximum of + 2.76 for caster, and allowable tolerances with a minimum of -0.24 and +1.24 for camber. Also, there is an allowable range for toe-in or toe-out, but preferred is a toe-in minimum of -1/16 inch with a maximum of 1/8 inch. The closer the buggy could be set to the preferred settings meant the better it would handle both while cornering and going straight.

My visual pre-adjustments resulted in these readouts on the alignment screen: Right side front, -0.24 caster with -0.51 camber and +5/8 toe-in; left side, +1.75 caster with +1.46 camber and +3/8 toe-in. All of my visual adjustments were not even close to the preferred or even the minimum settings.

Armed with all this information, Bob Varno proceeded to adjust the front toe-in plus the wheel caster and camber. After all front adjustments

Armed with all the information needed, Bob proceeded to adjust the front toe-in, plus the wheel caster and camber.

were made to the preferred settings, he then checked specifications and the actual adjustments for four-wheel alignment to make sure the rear wheels were adjusted properly (or, more simply, he was making sure all four wheels made a perfect square). The computer indicated the rear wheels were less than 1/16 of an inch out of adjustment. This is the true test of the quality of the used torsion arms we salvaged for the

buggy project. Less than 1/16 of an inch was not enough to justify loosening the rear torsion arms for adjustment.

After re-tightening all tie rod and camber locking nuts and reinstalling the hood, a road test was in order. And, the difference between the visually aligned front end and the computer alignment was like night and day. I could not believe how much better the buggy handled. No

more pulling right or left, no more wandering from side to side, and no more fighting the steering wheel for control.

This clearly demonstrated the importance of proper front end alignment performed by a professional technician with the right equipment. It proved to me that it is not possible for even the most experienced mechanic to guess at front wheel alignment and get it close. And, without proper front end alignment, there are a number of things that can and will happen, and they're all bad, ranging from uneven tire wear and premature tire failure to a vehicle that is virtually unsafe to drive on today's highways. ■

It took Bob less than an hour to bring the buggy's front end into spec. And what a difference it would make!

NOTES

_____

_____

_____

_____

_____

_____

_____

_____

_____

_____

_____

Installing a Skid Plate

Protecting Your Bottom

What is a skid plate? Most buggies don't even have one, but they all should, especially if they're used for serious off-roading. A skid plate is a very simple device, basically a flat metal plate that can be purchased over the counter or custom made. It can save a buggy owner the cost of a new engine.

Particularly vulnerable are the engine's push-rod tubes as they're exposed to stumps, rocks, etc. out on the trail, and road debris and extra deep chuck holes on the road. If you knock a hole in one of the eight push rod tubes or crack the block of the engine, you will shortly lose your oil and after it's gone, probably the engine.

Skid plates can be purchased that cover the entire underside of the engine and transmission. There are also types that bolt directly to the cylinder head exhaust studs and cover the push rod tubes only. I decided to design and install a skid plate that would be simple but fully protect both the bottom of the engine and the push rod tubes.

First, I measured the distance to the outside of the two support bars that hang down under the engine and that mount to the rear transmission bracket. This distance will vary from buggy to buggy and from frame to frame.

After I arrived at that measure-

Friend and VW expert Bob Supinger points out how vulnerable the engine's push-rod tubes are. They lay exposed to all sorts of dangers, such as rocks, stumps, tree limbs and chunks of debris that lay on the road.

ment, I added an extra four inches to the overall length (two inches per side) to ensure that I would clear the sides of the support bars. I then measured from that distance up to the bottom edge of the valve cover on each side and then added that to the total length of the piece. This gave me the overall length. I then measured the surface area that it would take to properly cover and protect the underside of the engine and push rod tubes. This gave me the width of the skid plate. I then gave these measurements to a metal fabrication shop and had a piece of hard aluminum

plate cut to size. There are different tensile strengths with aluminum and I opted for a hard aluminum for maximum protection.

Using the measurement I made going from the support bar to the valve cover, I measured that same distance in from each end of the skid plate. I then had the metal shop bend a 45-degree angle at that precise point on each side. Next, we held the plate up to the approximate location and checked for general clearance with the sides of the lower support bars.

We decided to fabricate and install a skid plate that would be simple in design and yet protect both the bottom of the engine and the push-rod tubes. First I measured the distance to the outside of the two support bars that hang down under the engine and that mount to the rear transmission bracket (arrows). Make sure you allow ample clearance beyond the sides of the support bars.

I then lowered the buggy off the hoist and used a floor jack to hold the skid plate in position while Bob Supinger centered it between the two lower support bars. After measuring an equal distance on each side and making sure it was far enough forward to properly cover the bottom of the engine and all the push-rod tubes, I marked this location with a magic marker. I then drilled holes through the skid plate and used common 1-1/2-inch muffler clamps in four separate locations to mount the skid plate to the lower support bars.

I used the standard muffler clamps to attach the skid plate instead of bolting directly to the lower support bars because I would have had to drill through the support bars and that could possibly weaken them.

With the new skid plate in place, my engine and push-rod tubes have vastly improved protection from the inherent dangers of the open road and trail. And I sleep a lot more soundly. ■

I then took these measurements to my local metal fabrication shop and had a piece of hard aluminum plate cut. There are different tensile strengths with aluminum and I opted for a hard aluminum for maximum protection.

With skid plate in hand, Bob raised the safety device into position.

Bob then checked thoroughly for proper clearance.

We then lowered the buggy off the hoist and used a floor jack to hold the skid plate into position while Bob centered it between the two lower support bars. After measuring an equal distance on each side and making sure the skid plate was far enough forward to properly cover the bottom of the engine and all the push-rod tubes, I marked this location with a magic marker.

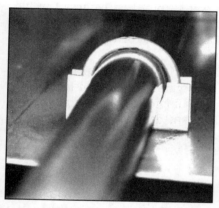

I then drilled holes through the skid plate and used common 1-1/2-inch muffler clamps to mount the skid plate.

Overall, we used four separate muffler clamps at four different locations to secure the skid plate to the lower support bars.

- VW Engine R... • Painting • Floor Pan
Suspension • Brakes & Options • Lights & Gauges
Transmission • Seats • Mounting Pedals • Steering
Emergency Cables • Fuel Tank • Skid Plate Clutch
Accessories • Body Panels • Engine Hop-Ups

ISBN 1-880524-26-0

9 781880 524268

90000

6 33769 00026